The Impatient Decorator

The Impatient Decorator

201 Shortcuts to a Beautiful Home

Glenna J. Morton

GLOUCESTER MASSACHUSETTS

ROCKPORT PUBLISHERS

First published in the United States of America by

Rockport Publishers, Inc.

33 Commercial Street

Gloucester, Massachusetts 01930-5089

Telephone: (978) 282-9590

Fax: (978) 283-2742

www.rockpub.com

Library of Congress Cataloging-in-Publication Data

Morton, Glenna.

  The impatient decorator: 201 shortcuts to a beautiful home/Glenna

Morton

   p. cm.

  ISBN 1-56496-960-6 (pbk.)

  1. House furnishings. 2. Interior decoration. I. Title.

TX311.M674 2003

747—dc21   2002153974

10 9 8 7 6 5 4 3 2 1

Design: Casey Design, Worcester, Massachusetts

Cover Images: Sam Gray/Garniture, York Show House 2001 (main image); courtesy of Laura Ashley, Ltd (left and right inset); courtesy of Calico Corners (middle inset)

Printed in Singapore

contents

Introduction

This book is for anyone who loves to decorate. You might feel, as I do, that few endeavors are as rewarding and enjoyable as creating attractive interiors for your own home. For us, decorating is not a destination but a journey of creativity.

You might be new to decorating—starting out with only some wedding gifts and a suitcase. You may be getting ready to move into your first apartment, first condo, or first home. Perhaps you've already moved several times and have accumulated lots of furnishings for your home.

No matter what stage you're at, however, more decorating challenges are right around the corner. We get married, divorced, and transferred; we also retire. New babies arrive, grow up, and go off to school. We move, remodel, and redecorate. Each of these events encourages us to rethink our surroundings, eliminate what doesn't work, and reinvent our living spaces to match our lifestyle.

The good news for today's home decorator is that much of the design world is now right at your doorstep. Quick access to the Internet makes it simple to get advice and information, to research, compare, and purchase almost anything for your home from anywhere in the world. Impatient decorators can even have the object of their dreams delivered to their door the very next day!

With countless resources at your fingertips, you have tremendous freedom to fashion uniquely personal spaces. You can just as easily design a room with animal-print fabrics and exotic masks as you can a pale blue room full of white Swedish furnishings. The choice is yours to **create any look you desire**—a concept that is as liberating as it can be intimidating.

Yet successful decorating is much more than a room full of fabrics, finishes, and furnishings. It is a balance of style with function and of comfort with personal expression. Designing a home takes a bit of **confidence** and a lot of **consistency**. It also takes **ideas** to solve each decorating challenge. When a design is right, it provides useful spaces for all of life's activities and pleases us every day.

Teach yourself more about decorating by taking more notice of design. Look at store displays, collect decorating books, visit designer showhouses, and study the pages of decorating magazines and Web sites.

Evaluate each style idea, color, and furniture arrangement you encounter. Ask yourself, "Do I like this? Why? How would I do this differently? How many colors are used? What's the inspiration for this room? What activities take place here? Does it work?" You'll find yourself becoming more discerning about design. You'll also develop a better understanding of your own preferences.

Continue your decorating journey with the **201 decorating tips** in this book. Use each idea as a springboard for your own creativity. Embellish them with a personal twist so the idea is no longer "from a book" but your very own.

A serene bedroom in white, sage, and sand harmonizes elegance and comfort without distracting from the room's spectacular ocean view.

Five Ways to Get More from This Book

While this book can be read from start to finish, it can also be browsed time and again to glean ideas for ongoing decorating projects. Here are several ways to get the most out of this book.

1. **Working on a decorating project right now?** Turn to the tips aimed at the specific room you're decorating—the bedroom, dining room, kitchen, or hall.

2. **Need help with the basics?** Look for the chapters on paint, color, fabrics, lighting, and window treatments, as these topics pertain to most decorating projects.

3. **Uncertain about your style preferences?** Browse the photographs in this book for rooms you like and mark them with a bookmark or selfstick note. Study each picture, noting what you like and what you don't. This exercise can help zero in on your personal style.

4. **Looking for a specific room element?** Search for photographs and ideas that relate. You might look for window treatments one day and furniture arrangements another, trolling for ideas that are just right for your project.

5. **Want color options?** The photographs in this book represent a variety of color schemes. Step into each of these rooms for a moment. Do the colors encourage you to feel happy, serene, or bland? Knowing how you respond to certain colors can help determine which hues you'll want to bring into your home.

Just want to know more about decorating? Read the entire book and begin banking ideas into your own database of decorating inspiration.

Be sure to pick up this book—and other favorite decorating books—from time to time. As your taste and decorating talents evolve, new ideas, new solutions will appear with each examination, and you'll be able to draw on them for every decorating project.

Looking for Decorating Inspiration on the Internet

- www.bhg.com
- www.homestore.com/Decorate/default.asp
- www.ivillage.com/home
- interiordec.about.com

Chapter 1

Color

What's your favorite color? Ask a child and you'll get an immediate response. "Red," she might say, or "It used to be pink, but now I like purple!"

An adult's passion for color is sometimes harder to pinpoint. Advertising and the media promote the newest color forecasts for each season, tempting us to add the latest trendy hues to our homes.

But let's forget about the media, the forecasts, and the trends. Forget that article you read about all-white rooms. Overlook the neutrals that fill department store shelves, and don't give a second thought to retro, nouveau, or deco hues. So, really, what is your favorite color, anyway?

Just to get the ball rolling, I'll tell you my favorite color: it's blue. I've always known that, yet through the years I've tried rooms in brown, beige, green, and pink. Even though those rooms were lovely, I wasn't completely satisfied with my home's color until I returned to blue.

Most likely you already recognize the color that entices you again and again. It might be strawberry red, leafy green, or sunny yellow. It might be misty beige, snowflake white, or foggy gray. It's the color that beckons you in shop windows, fabric stores, and magazine photos. It's the one you'd most like to see when you open your eyes in the morning, the one that prompts you to say, "I love that!"

If you're lucky, you've already decorated your home with "your" color and, if not, then maybe it's time for a change.

The influence of color extends well beyond our personal reactions, however. It's well known that yellows warm and brighten, reds stimulate and excite, while restful blues calm and cool us.

We've heard that bright color appears to advance while pale tones and neutrals feel open and airy. We've observed that dark hues bring the walls closer, making spaces feel cozy. Thus, we know it's possible to employ the traits of color to alter our perception of space.

Yet the properties of color count for less than your attraction to a particular color. A totally red room that feels overpowering to some people will be your favorite room in the house—if you adore red. An all-white room that seems airy and unanchored to others might be your own serene, romantic retreat.

There are so many ways to use color in a home that it's easy to feel overwhelmed with choices. Do you paint the walls with color, like the room on page 66? Should you totally immerse a room in saturated color, like the living room on page 38? Can you highlight a color by using it only for accents, like the blue sconces on page 68? Will you place the color on both the floor and the furniture, as on page 61?

The answer, of course, is that *all* of these techniques can be employed to bring color into your home. Go neutral in one room to show off colored accessories. Go saturated with cozy color in another room. Do rugs in your color in one location and use it on upholstered furniture in another. Spreading your color around links the spaces in your home and adds to the impression of decorating harmony.

Another advantage of a consistent color scheme is that whenever you make changes in your current home or move to a new home, you can redistribute your furnishings to new locations knowing the colors will work. That may be the smartest color technique of them all.

So which color did you say was your favorite?

The colorful red valance adds life to a small attic space and frames the pretty window detail.

Create cool serenity with a palette of white and a few vintage accessories.

Color

#1
You Are the Boss of Color

Learn more about color by browsing photographs in decorating books and magazines. As you view a room scene, note the main color, secondary color, and accent colors—where they come from and how they are distributed throughout a space. Do they share similar values (all pale or all deep)? Which colors draw your interest? Which seem dull? These observations can put you in charge of your own color schemes.

#2
The Value of Color

Colors that share a similar value in **tint** (lightness) or **shade** (darkness) can be the start of harmonious color schemes. For example, pale pink is a tint of red. Its light color value means it will **work well with other light colors**, including pale blue, yellow, and lavender. Grab a few paint chips and compare the lightest choice on each card. See how well they combine?

#3
Put Your Color Scheme in Writing

Avoid a disjointed look in your home by taking the time to **spell out a definite color scheme**. Write down exactly which color will be used as the main color, the secondary color, and the accent colors in each room. This makes shopping easier and gives you a blueprint for color choices. Remember, **defining a color scheme** is easier when it's inspired by fabric or pattern (see tip #7 for details).

#4
Give Color a Reason

Sometimes the challenge of an older home involves working around a few unattractive elements—a green bathtub, pink tile, or brown linoleum. One of the ways to deal with **an existing color** you can't replace right away is to use a bit *more* of that color in the room. Choosing fabrics and patterns that include the color give it a reason for being in the room.

Brilliant orange and blue accents dazzle in a space defined by cool gray and white. The accessories of metal and glass resonate with shimmering white silk panels at the windows.

Color

#5

Any Color + White = Crisp

Pairing almost any color with white offers a look that's easy and timeless. **Classic schemes** include blue and white (page 25), black and white (page 85), and red and white (page 13), but think beyond the norm to use your own favorites—perhaps seafoam, cantaloupe, kiwi, mushroom, goldenrod, or sunset pink. Repeat your chosen color, and the white, throughout the room.

#6

Direct the Eye

Use color to direct the eye to the best features of a room. Subtle colors tend to stay in the background, yielding center stage to brighter accessories or a great view. Bright colors, on the other hand, draw our attention and might be used to highlight the best features or furnishings in a room—a beautiful chair, gorgeous area rug, or lovely mantle area. It makes sense then, to refrain from using brights where extra importance isn't warranted, like radiators, pipes, or any other less-than-perfect details.

#7

Learn One Formula

While there are **many ways to construct a color scheme**, a basic three-color formula is one of the easiest. Take three colors from a fabric, a rug, or an object, such as a painting or vase. Distribute them as follows:

60–70 percent of the room in the main color, usually the lightest and often applied to the walls

20–30 percent of the room in the secondary color, sometimes a midtone and used on upholstered furniture

10 percent of the room in the accent color, usually the brightest, seen in the room's accessories

#8

Warm or Cool—It's Your Call

Almost every **color has undertones that are warm** (leaning toward red or yellow) **or cool** (with more blue or green). Look for these nuances when shopping for paint, fabric, or furnishings. Beige, for instance, may be rosy or tan. Pink can show up as a warm peachy pink or a cool bluish pink. Greens might be a yellow avocado green or a blue teal green. Even white and ivory have highlights of color, so choose carefully when matching colors or deciding on the color direction for a room.

Simple white furniture, seagrass flooring, and a trio of coordinated fabrics are grounded by a handful of darker accent pieces.

A strong wall color based on the patterned rug supports
the intense hues of the artwork and warms the space.

Color

#9
Work with Rug Colors

A patterned carpet or rug is often **the starting point in a room**; in this case, choose a color scheme that blends with the rug's colors. Because most rugs can't be carried with you as you shop, spread out a handful of paint chips and identify colors that match the rug. Put the chips in your shopping kit; a photograph of the rug is another useful addition.

#10
Offset Deep Color with Lighter Tones

Balance rich color by using lighter hues in other areas of the room. The terra-cotta walls in the picture on this page are important, yet not overpowering, because the furniture and trims are pale. The bonus of using colors on the walls is that updating the look of the room by repainting it is fairly simple, whereas reupholstering furniture to update a color is neither simple nor inexpensive.

#11
Soften the Brights

Eye-popping color creates instant excitement. What do you do, however, if a bright color you've chosen suddenly seems like *too much*? For a painted surface, test an area to see if colorwashing over too-bright paint (with slightly diluted neutral paint) tones it down. Paint stores can also supply aging glazes to soften the look of bright walls, painted furniture, and wallpaper. Fabrics can sometimes be dipped in tea or faded in the sun to develop a more timeworn appearance.

#12
Repeat after Me...

Always distribute color throughout a room. Placing color in only one area can look like an afterthought, so aim to **display every color in at least three places** in the room. The living room on pages 68-69 is a good example. Notice how little blue is in the room, yet its repetition in two sconces and the vase seems satisfying. Remember: *Repetition doth a color scheme make.*

Chapter 2

Fabric

Many great room schemes start with fabric. Once the inspirational fabric is selected, it can be scrutinized for color, formality, and style. These clues help shape the décor of the whole room.

From fresh florals to tailored stripes, we love the look, the feel, and the style of fabric, the endless variety and utility of which is easy to appreciate. Fabric can be stretched, draped, sewn, glued, swagged, and stapled. We can sit on it, hang it, or sleep on it—thus, fabric is one of the most flexible elements in a home.

The appeal of fabric is as universal as its origins. Luscious silks, crisp cottons, soft wools, and textured linens—from China, India, Ireland, New Zealand, England, Scandinavia, and more—are vibrant with color, pattern, and texture. Base a color scheme on one of these fabrics and you'll have instant focus and direction for a decorating project.

Home fabric stores and drapery workrooms are terrific sources of fabrics, ideas, and labor. In addition to a wide selection of the newest textiles and colors, you'll also find linings, trims, pillow forms, and drapery hardware.

Anyone who sews sees endless possibilities in these aisles of colorful yard goods and gravitates naturally toward starting a room with fabric, knowing a flat piece of yardage can be turned into fluffy pillows, elegant draperies, tablecloths, slipcovers, duvet covers, and more.

Yet just as many fabric projects can be undertaken by those who don't sew a stitch. Hot glue,

Coordinated fabric collections make it simple to enliven a color scheme.

staple guns, iron-on fusible webbing, fabric glues, and other products make it easy for anyone to fashion personalized fabric items for a room. In addition, lampshade and roller shade kits supply do-it-yourselfers with everything needed to make those items.

Whether you sew or not, professional workrooms are always available to create almost anything you can dream up. Though custom work requires a larger budget, it offers a look that's unmatched.

In sum, next time you're thinking about redoing a room, take your inspiration, your colors, and your style cues from fabric.

Plain upholstery fabric pairs easily with stripes and prints and can be revitalized from season to season by varying the pillows and accessories.

Fabric

#13
Get the Knack for Coordinating Patterns

The trick to using patterns in a room is to **pay attention to style, color, and scale**. Choose fabrics that are similar in formality—in other words, don't try to pair materials as incompatible as burlap and satin. In addition, look for a range of prints that **share a few common colors**, like the fabrics shown here. Finally, include a mix of **large, medium, and small prints** along with one or two plain or textured fabrics.

#14
Choose One Fabric for Inspiration

When using several coordinated fabrics, choose one of them as the **primary fabric in a room**. Often, you'll find a fabric that includes so many colors that you'll be able to use it as the inspiration for your entire home, pulling out colors in various combinations for each room. Although no one formula works for every project, learning to base a color scheme on fabric is a terrific way to start a decorating project.

Designer-coordinated lines of fabric are an excellent resource for the impatient decorator. The yellow floral shown here sets the tone, and the harmonizing large, medium, and small prints echo its colors in different combinations.

#15
Adorn the Seams

Add a braid, cording, fringe, or other **dressmaker trim** to the seams where two fabrics meet—along the edges of double-sided drapery panels, outlining a pillow, or on the perimeter of a duvet cover. If expensive trims aren't your choice, a simple corded fabric welt made of a contrasting stripe, check, or plain fabric will add interest on a budget.

#16
Save the Scraps

Don't have enough leftover fabric to make a tablecloth or bedskirt? Try patchwork! However, instead of sewing small squares together, join **wide fabric strips**. Sew sections of leftovers next to plain or coordinating fabric. Once the pieces are stitched and ironed flat, cut out a tablecloth, bedskirt, or pillow front. This piecing method can also be used to create a custom look for draperies and slipcovers.

Looking for Fabric Ideas on the Internet
- www.waverly.com
- www.calicocorners.com
- www.marimekko.com
- www.lauraashley.com

Fabric

#17
Prewash for Softness

If you've selected a washable fabric in the hopes of tossing it into the laundry from time to time, you may want to **consider washing fabric before making it up**. This should minimize future shrinkage problems. Slipcovers, tablecloths, shams, pillows, and runners are all candidates for this treatment. Test wash a yard or two before committing to washing an entire bolt. If laundering isn't satisfactory, dry cleaning may offer better results.

#18
Make Decorating Elements Reversible

An easy way to **change the look of a room** is to design reversible soft goods. Pillows, comforters, table toppers, and even simple slipcovers can be made with one fabric on one side and a coordinating pattern on the opposite side, allowing simple seasonal transitions. Flat panel or rod pocket drapes also reverse if they are sewn in a pillowcase style. Add a finishing touch with a narrow flange, fringe, or cording sewn into the seams between the front and back fabrics.

#19
Stripes and Checks Can Live Anywhere

When you've identified a patterned fabric as your inspiration, look for stripes, checks, or geometric designs to partner with it. These **multipurpose prints** make excellent accent fabrics and are especially useful for lining, borders, cording, tabs, and ties. In addition running a stripe horizontally, vertically, or diagonally allows a number of looks from the same fabric.

#20
Protect Fabrics from Fading

The sun's ultraviolet (UV) rays can quickly fade fabrics and weaken fibers. To avoid this, **protect all fabric, upholstery, and rugs** in your home. Tilt blinds (or draw lined draperies closed) during the daylight hours to keep sun from shining directly on textiles. If you prefer to leave windows uncovered, consider exterior awnings, or install tinted film directly onto the window glass to filter out harmful UV rays.

Draperies lined with a coordinating print fall from ceiling to floor in a pattern that inspires a soft blue and white color scheme.

Fabric

#21
Be Frugal with Expensive Fabric

Have you ever fallen in love with expensive fabric only to find the cost makes it impractical to purchase as much as you'd planned? Get creative! Buy less—and **use it as your room's inspiration**. Use less-costly plain fabric for large items like upholstery, drapery, and slipcovers, then distribute the higher-priced fabric throughout the room in projects that require minimal yardage—borders, welting, valances, tiebacks, pillows, runners, table toppers, chair seats, or lampshades.

#22
Heat Up the Iron

Never use fabric in your home without ironing it. Rumpled and creased bedskirts and curtain panels practically shout that you neglected to take a few extra minutes to do it right. Iron everything that comes out of a package as well as everything you make yourself. It's one absolutely free detail that can make the least inexpensive item look terrific. When concerned about heat damage, read the label and test press a fabric scrap or an inconspicuous area.

#23
Keep Control of Your Project

Ordering custom work such as draperies, duvet covers, pillows, and upholstery gives your rooms one-of-a-kind detail. However, don't assume you can drop off the fabric at the workroom and forget about it. Here are points to keep in mind:

• Always double-check measurements.

• Ask the workroom to return large scraps and all extra fabric.

• On multimotif toiles and other large-print fabrics, choose what you consider the main pattern and note it on the order.

• Determine how fabric should be placed and which pattern motifs belong at the top, bottom, or center of furnishings.

• Clearly specify in the contract that patterns will be exactly matched at all seams; this is particularly crucial for striped fabric.

• Consider specialized linings, headings, and finishing details, like cording and fringes, which may enhance the finished product.

Lustrous silk fabric radiates with a pearly sheen on panels designed to wrap the head of the bed in luxury.

Chapter 3

Furniture

Most of us already own an assortment of furniture. We may like it all, or none of it. It may work well for us, or perhaps its function could be improved. We may love the style and color of our furnishings, or we may wish we could start over.

Ideally, our furniture is a reflection of our creativity, interests, and personality. It ought to fit into our rooms, offer comfortable seating or useful storage, and move with us to new locations. It should be interesting enough to catch our eye but classic and well-made to endure for years. If that isn't too tall an order, it also needs to be affordable on our budget.

Furnishing a house is a major investment in both money and time and, thus, one that should be thoughtfully considered. While impulse purchases are sometimes fortuitous, hasty decisions can result in disappointment when we later find a different piece that might have been a smarter choice.

The furniture you choose will likely be a part of your life for a long time. It costs you something in terms of money, space, and maintenance yet offers valuable returns on your investment by providing function and beauty.

The global and eclectic styles so prevalent today bring together a mix of furniture that appears to have been collected over time. To develop this look, avoid buying matched suites of furniture where every piece is the same color and material. Instead, look for pieces that offer one-of-a-kind style.

Most room projects will benefit from a **measured floor plan drawing**. This is a bird's-eye view of the room drawn to scale on grid paper. **Elevation drawings** (a face-on sketch of each wall) show measurements and the placement of windows, doors, and other features. Make photocopies of your floorplans and elevations and draw all over them with furniture ideas, notes, and layouts. Take them shopping and refer to them when making initial judgments about whether or not a certain piece of furniture will fit into your space.

A good place to begin looking for furniture is right in your own home. Take a thoughtful inventory of what you have and make a list of things you need or want. **Focus first on problems and solutions**. Do you need a desk, more filing space, a comfortable upholstered chair, or a good reading light? Such unfilled needs can be daily annoyances until they are addressed.

If you're decorating on a dime, find ways to rescue, refurbish, or recycle tired furnishings. Look for consignment stores, garage sales, flea markets, and auctions where furniture can be a bargain. Trade furniture with friends, or build a few things yourself. Projects like plywood- or glass-topped tables need little more expertise than carting home a circular or rectangular top and setting it on a sturdy base.

As you consider the furniture you'll place in your home, **dare to imagine something different**. How would it feel to put the desk on an angle, move the bed to a different wall, or turn a boxy, unused bedroom into a library? What if you threw out your tired sofa and arranged four comfortable upholstered chairs in a circle in the living room? How would it work to move your favorite chair in front of a sunny window or the dining room table facing the fireplace?

Innovations like these can have surprising and happy results. Once you start to think creatively about furniture, you'll find new solutions and possibilities around every corner.

Chests are the perfect marriage of beauty and utility and are at home in just about any room.

Furniture

An armoire is a strong presence in a space and can be used to balance the visual weight of other room features such as fireplaces and built-ins.

#24
Choose Classic Workhorses

Armoires, bookcases, and chests of drawers are tried-and-true classics that earn their keep. **Buy pieces you love**. As you move from home to home, they'll adapt to work in a variety of locations. A chest, for example, can serve as an entry table in one home, a night-stand in another, and a sideboard somewhere else. An armoire might hold china in a dining room, clothing in a bedroom, an entertainment center in a family room, or a home office in a guest room.

#25
Think Storage

Get more from furniture purchases by looking for pieces that offer storage as well as style. This is a great way to **pack more storage into smaller homes**. Instead of choosing a sofa table on four legs, look for a cabinet with doors. A small shelf in the entry might be replaced with a more useful chest of drawers, while floor space reserved for an open bookcase might be better used for an armoire that incorporates closed storage.

Versatile nesting tables multiply your furniture options, especially in a small space.

#26
Nest, Separate, Stack

Occasional furnishings that nest, separate, or stack are versatile and can be **reconfigured as needs change**. A must-have for small homes, nesting tables function admirably as one nested unit, or they can be separated to use individually for entertaining. Push a pair of ottomans together as a coffee table or assign them to separate rooms. Stacking shelves or cubes can also be flexible components of creative storage solutions.

#27
Do-It-Yourself
Glass-Topped Tables

Glass tabletops (like the one on page 79) **pair easily** with any sturdy base, including stone pedestals, columns, benches, plant pots, and wooden boxes. How about a glass-topped octagonal side table, rectangular hall table, or large square dining table? Add elegant detail with beveled edges and rounded corners. Use glass thick enough for your table's size and be conservative with the diameter; the top may be unstable if it extends too far beyond the perimeter of the base.

Furniture

#28
Choose Your Own "Neutrals" for Upholstery

Plain, neutral fabric is a terrific, long-lasting choice for upholstered items. Beige and tan are suitable options, if that's your style. If not, then create your own neutrals—that is, the **colors that show up as basics** in your decorating scheme. Whether you choose pale gold, sage green, chocolate brown, or navy blue, using **plain textured fabrics** in your colors ensures that upholstered pieces will have a long and useful life.

#29
Furniture Beauty Is More than Skin Deep

When designers advise "get the best you can afford," it's because **quality lasts**! The slogan "you get what you pay for" definitely applies. A cheaply made sofa, no matter how attractive the fabric covering, can sag, rumple, and turn lumpy within a year. Instead, buy superior construction details like kiln-dried hardwoods and eight-way hand-tied springs—*then* find the right upholstery fabric.

#30
Add Texture with Accent Pieces

A great way to introduce texture into a room is to add pieces made of **carved wood, wicker, rattan, or bamboo**, which contribute not only texture but an eclectic and international feel. Look for Chinese stacking baskets, antique wicker chairs, or an Asian bamboo table. Visit import stores for carved Moroccan panels, rattan bookshelves, and versatile metal tray tables.

Looking for Furniture on the Internet
- www.kohlerinteriors.com
- www.furnitureguide.com
- www.furniturefan.com
- www.room.se

A classic comfort piece—a soft chair—beckons at the end of a long day.

A handful of rosy pink pillows and accents of Chinese export porcelain add character to a room of furniture sheathed in white slipcovers.

Furniture

#31
Slipcovers Camouflage and Update

Rescue almost any group of **mismatched upholstered furniture** by slipcovering each piece in the same fabric. **Ready-made** covers are inexpensive but may not fit every piece. **Semicustom** covers, made to your measurements, are offered by some Internet sources. Most expensive are **custom-made** covers that fit your furniture perfectly. Custom sewing also provides infinite options in fabrics and finishing details as well a choice of styles, from tailored to loose.

#32
Use Paint to Rescue Wood Furniture

Revive unattractive wood furniture with a **fresh painted finish**. White painted furniture is appropriate for cottage- and Swedish-style rooms, while black unites with a European or Asian flair. However, any color you choose—yellow, red, navy, ivory, or others—can land a color punch. If you wish, layer on more personality with stenciling, decoupage, or painted accent designs. For a vintage look, try a top coat of crackle medium, or apply an aging technique.

#33
Color Can Highlight or Hide

Fall back on an old decorator's trick to make tiny rooms appear larger by **matching the furnishings to a pale wall color**. Against a yellow wall, for instance, a chest will look less imposing when painted a similar yellow. This technique is perfect for a child's room where space is limited and the colors in toys and books compete for attention.

Chapter 4 Lighting

More often than not, too little attention is paid to lighting. Typical homes are built with ceiling fixtures and electrical outlets and offer little lighting creativity. Newer homes may include recessed lighting in the kitchen and strip lights over a bathroom mirror, but the effect may be equally unimaginative.

With minimal electrical requirements in place, we tend to focus attention on carpet, furniture, window treatments, and paint. Then, once the room is decorated, we plug in a couple of lamps and call it done.

Yet lighting is one element that can make or break the look of a room. Without it, we're in the dark—literally. Done well, it creates ambience and drama and offers the functional illumination we need for living.

When a space is fully decorated but still seems lifeless and uninteresting, sometimes the answer is to **layer in more light**. Focus light on art, plants, and collectibles. Wash the walls in light with recessed fixtures. Add strip lights to bookshelves. Create attention-grabbing zones of illumination on a focal point, tables, or sculpture. You may find your dull room rejuvenated.

A **mix of lighting types** provides multiple lighting options. You might dim the overhead lighting for a party, turn it up for a neighborhood meeting, or turn it off altogether for a fireside dinner. You can illuminate display shelves in one part of the room and switch on reading lights in another. The **areas of light and shadow,** created by a range of light sources, enhance the room's ambiance and interest.

Adding more fixtures to an existing home can be a challenge. A qualified electrician may be required for some retrofit installations. Inquire with your local building or planning department regarding code questions and to determine whether permits or inspections are required for a particular electrical project. Other projects simply require problem solving and the careful selection of appropriate fixtures to fit existing spaces.

For new home construction, it's wise to begin lighting plans early in the design process. Visit lighting showrooms and hire a lighting designer to identify the best solutions possible for your new home. Pay careful attention not only to the fixtures but to their locations and the placement and convenience of the corresponding switches. Also, consider including extra fixtures and outlets to accommodate hobby equipment, special appliances, and holiday lighting.

Where furniture will be arranged in the middle of a large room—focused around the fireplace, for example—ask your architect to designate floor boxes so lamps can easily be plugged in under the furniture.

Here are other locations where outlets or fixtures can be convenient:

- at the back of a television niche

- next to the mantle for holiday lights

- in a walk-in closet for an iron or steamer

- in a hallway for a vacuum or table lamp

- near windows for seasonal light displays

- underneath upper cabinets, for countertop lighting

- inside cabinets with glass doors

- inside every closet, with an automatic on/off switch controlled by the door

- braced ceiling boxes for paddle fans

- recessed lighting over beds for reading

- wall sconces over mantles, in halls, and next to bathroom mirrors

Dramatic pools of light from contemporary fixtures draw attention to each important area in this room: the seating area, fireplace, artwork, and display shelves at the far end.

Four types of light—a chandelier, recessed ceiling fixtures, sconces, and candlelight— make this living room glow.

Lighting

#34
Chandeliers Aren't Just for the Dining Room

Chandeliers offer such romantic lighting; why confine them to the dining room? How about using one in the master bedroom (page 142), living room, foyer, or kitchen (page 106)? The inviting presence of a chandelier will add a touch of elegance to grand rooms as well as to more mundane spaces, like hallways or master bathrooms.

- Hang a chandelier 30 to 36 inches (76 to 91 cm) above a dining room table.

- Hang a chandelier in hallway locations at least 80 inches (2 m) off the floor to allow ample headroom.

- Allow 8 to 12 inches (20 to 30 cm) of clearance between the perimeter of the chandelier and the table edges underneath—thus, a table 4 feet (122 cm) wide accommodates a light fixture about 2 feet (61 cm) across.

- Hang two chandeliers or pendant lights over a rectangular dining table to accentuate its length.

#35
Install a Ceiling Medallion

Medallions are a simple way to add a touch of elegance to a room. They are attached to the ceiling *before* installing the chandelier. Available in styles from plain to elaborate, you'll also find a choice of diameters from 12 to 40 inches (30 to 102 cm). Visit a lighting store or browse online for information, photographs, and sizing tips.

#36
Camouflage Chandelier Chains

A simple fabric sleeve will cover the chandelier's **exposed chain and cord**. Sew a narrow tube twice as long as the chain and sized to fit around the chain's diameter. Turn it right-side out, iron flat, and slip the sleeve over the chain and cord prior to wiring the fixture into the electrical box on the ceiling. Adjust gathers and tuck raw edges inside.

#37
Lighting Is in the Details

Take advantage of the many **lighting products** available that help focus light and add control.

- Add dimmer switches to ceiling fixtures and lamps.

- Install picture lights to highlight artwork.

- Use motion-detector light switches in laundry rooms and garages.

- Set uplights in corners, behind plants, and on top of armoires.

- Use undercabinet lights, bookcase strip lights, and specialty fixtures to shine light where you need it.

Lighting

#38
Dare to Pair

Pairs of lamps add a pleasing symmetry as well as warm light. The small footprint of elegant, tall candlestick-style lamps, also known as buffet lamps, takes up little space on a tabletop, leaving plenty of room for decorative accessories. Place the lamps at either end of a sideboard, mantle, or dressing table for classic sophistication.

#39
Height Matters

Your room will have a more harmonious look **if you stick with one or two lamp-shade heights**. If necessary, boost shorter table lamps by placing them on a decorative box or stack of books. A matching pair of table lamps is another good solution when they are set on surfaces of equal height. Adjustable floor lamps can make height adjustments a breeze.

#40
Play Dress Up with Shades

Pretty up plain lampshades by trimming the top or bottom edges with decorative cording, braid, or fringe attached with low-temperature hot glue or fabric glue. Some trims are best attached to the outside of the shade. Others, like ropes of beads or crystals with one unfinished edge, should be glued inside the lower rim of the shade, leaving the decorative trim to peek out underneath.

#41
Create a Do-It-Yourself Lamp

Did you know you can make a lamp out of nearly any decorative object? Take a favorite accessory—a wooden box, vase, tin box, trophy, or urn—to a lamp shop, where they can drill the item and wire it with lamp parts. The result is a **one-of-a-kind lamp** in just the right size, shape, and color for your room.

The symmetry of a matching pair of lamps underscores the formality of this bedroom and imbues the monochromatic color scheme with additional warmth.

Focused overhead track fixtures point light precisely where it is needed along the length of the kitchen counters.

Lighting

#42
Get on Board with Track Lights

A good solution for room makeovers, **track lighting is easily installed** in existing ceiling outlets and can be updated with more fixtures as needed. Experiment with the angle of the fixtures to find positions that contribute both task illumination and dramatic pools of light on artwork or countertops. Use dimmer switches to control the intensity of light.

#43
Go Wild with Uplights

Purchase inexpensive uplights (basically metal cans with a floodlight inside) online, in lighting stores, or at home centers. Set them in corners, behind plants, and on top of tall armoires where they'll increase illumination and cast interesting shadows.
Note: Make sure kids, pets, and hanging draperies won't interfere with the heat of the lights.

#44
Tame Cord Tangles

Electrical cords can detract from the beauty of a room. **Control cord clutter** by running wires under furniture, close to table legs, or neatly along baseboards. Cords may be made less obtrusive by replacing them with new cords that are clear, white, or dark. Buy these in exactly the right length to eliminate bulky extension cords.

#45
Fan the Summer Away

Installing a ceiling fan is a great way to **cool off in the heat of summer**. Look for models that include a remote control (or buy a remote kit separately) that is installed into the fan's electrical box *before* it is wired to the ceiling. To coordinate a fan with a colorful room, purchase a plain style and paint or stencil the blades to match.

Looking for Lighting on the Internet
- www.shades-of-light.com
- www.lampsplus.com
- www.bellacor.com
- www.americanlightingassoc.com

Chapter 5 Paint

You're not alone if your first thought is to run out and buy a couple of gallons of paint as soon as you've decided to decorate a room.

In truth, however, paint is not the first item that should be purchased for a room. As one of **the most flexible decorating elements**, it can easily be fine-tuned *after* fabrics, flooring, and furniture have been chosen.

The good news is that paint comes in hundreds, even thousands, of colors, so any color can be matched, contrasted, or coordinated fairly easily. The bad news is that paint sometimes has fickle undertones of color that respond to a room's available light sources.

Don't think you're off the color-choice hook because you want beige, as some beiges lean toward pink, others to gold, gray, or green in their undertone.

How to choose **the right shade for your project**? Once you've settled on the other room elements, begin to sort through paint chips.

When your project requires a light paint color, be sure to **look at all the shades on** a paint strip to see where the color is "going" before you buy. You might notice, for instance, that the deeper shades on the Starlight Beige paint card turn muddy instead of golden. This undertone may be present in the lighter paints as well. The fix? Browse the rack for deeper colors with just the right tones and see if the lighter samples on those cards work for your project.

Choose three paint possibilities and buy the smallest quantity of each, along with a pint of white paint. The paints you test might be completely different colors, or they could be similar colors from different manufacturers.

Paint large squares on the wall—the larger the better. If it's impractical to paint on the wall, then paint an entire sheet of inexpensive **white poster board** from a stationery or craft store. Brush the paint on with a foam roller or pad painter, let dry, and add a second coat if necessary. Tack this up in the room and bring in all of the flooring and fabric samples, plus accessories, so you can view everything together.

If the paint samples are deeper in color than you like, try lighter shades by mixing in measured quantities of the white paint and doing more sample boards. (Keep the poster board with your final paint choice and cut it into sample- and wallet-size pieces to carry with you when purchasing other home décor items.)

Always view samples on the same plane as the finished product—that is, look at paint samples vertically, as on a wall. View flooring samples set on the floor. Look at everything—the paint samples, fabrics, flooring, etc.—in the room in several locations to get the full effect of how the colors behave in the brightest as well as the most shaded areas.

Check the colors throughout the day and at night under artificial lighting conditions. A clear winner will usually emerge. If not, go back to your paint chips and try again.

Many homeowners have second thoughts about a paint color once it is actually up on the wall. It might seem too bright, too intense, too dull, or just not the way they thought it would look. Before repainting, however, allow some time to get used to it. Bring in the furniture and accessories. Often, seeing everything in context shows that yes, it all goes perfectly together, just as you planned.

Paint

#46
Diversify Paint Choices

Collect paint chips from various brands before deciding which shades to try in your home. Each manufacturer employs a different formulation, which means every color—even those that look similar on a paint chip—has different undertones and highlights. If the paint brand and dealer are not printed on the card, add this information to the back of each color strip to avoid losing track of where you picked up the samples.

#47
View Paint Colors with Other Samples

When matching paint chips to a fabric, flooring, or existing paint finish, try placing the chips **underneath or behind** the item, if possible, rather than on top of it. Sort through the chips, discarding the colors that are obviously not a match. Then cut apart the finalists, noting the color, brand, and store on the back. Hold them above and below your samples under various light conditions before choosing a few to test on the wall.

#48
Match Anything with Paint Chips

Use paint chips as **stand-in samples** of items in your home that are fixed in place or too large to carry around, such as carpeting, tile, or an existing paint finish. You might, for example, want to find fabric to go with your sage green bathroom tile. Collect a handful of green paint chips and match one to the tile. Mark this chip "tile" and take it with you whenever you are shopping for other items for your room.

#49
Paint Covers Almost Everything

There's a paint for every purpose. Take any color problem to a paint dealer and you'll likely find products to help. Old kitchen cabinets, flea market furniture, and dingy ceilings are just a few of the makeover opportunities paint can handle. Metals are also good candidates for paint fixes, so go ahead and buy that bargain dark metal garage sale chandelier and spray paint it into a lovely white swan of a fixture.

Rich terra-cotta paint enfolds the walls in color and contrasts with the striking black and white accents on the stairway, fabrics, and furnishings.

Paint

#50
Tint Your Primer

A primer can easily be tinted to resemble almost any light paint color. Though tinted primer may not exactly match the top coat, any slight difference in color may make it easier to distinguish between coats when you are actually painting. Most dark colors cannot be matched in primer, but tinting may improve coverage compared to using white primer.

#51
Painting the Details

While you're painting your room, take note of the grates, vents, outlet covers, radiators, and pipes. These will be **less noticeable when they're painted the same color** as the wall behind them. If in doubt about painting a removable object, take it to a paint store to ask if a primer or other finish is needed. *Note: Experts advise against painting smoke detectors.*

#52
Paint a Floor

Change the color of an unattractive concrete, vinyl, or wood floor with paint. Get advice for your particular project from a paint dealer. Most floors should be thoroughly cleaned and primed first (use a stain-killing primer to keep old finishes from seeping through). Top coat with your chosen color and, if desired, apply stencils, borders, checkerboards, or faux techniques. Finally, apply several layers of clear polyurethane and allow to dry thoroughly.

Paint is featured everywhere in this happy child's room—from sunny yellow walls to the whimsically cut-out headboard and built-ins.

#53
Highlight with Paint

Show off the unique outlines and details of furniture with paint. In the room on this page, hot pink defines the undulating curves of the headboard, the arched panels on the window seat, and the crown molding of the green bookcase. These small areas are eye-catching bursts of color that echo the pink in the floral fabric.

Paint

#54
Love Rich Color? Give It a Starring Role!

Don't be afraid of using a **color you really love**. Dark, deep, or bright wall colors can make a room feel instantly decorated. Balance these colors with liberal splashes of lighter tones, white, or ivory on the trim and ceilings. Carefully consider furniture colors as well. Light furniture pops when set in front of richly colored walls.

#55
Use Contrast for Interest

Color can be enhanced when it's skillfully combined with a contrasting hue. For drama, use a **high-contrast** color scheme, such as bright white trim in a room with navy walls, or walnut wood doors next to walls the color of beach sand. For a subtler touch, try **low-contrast combinations**, such as white with pale green or butter yellow with ivory.

#56
Create a Glow from Above

Take a cue from gracious plantation porches and verandas by **painting a ceiling** a beautiful sky blue, aqua, pale peach, blush pink, or soft golden yellow. Such ceilings are intrinsically interesting, and the right shade of paint can impart a flattering glow. Test ceiling colors with wall colors by sampling them together in the room. Remember that ceilings are usually seen in shadow and tend to look darker, so ceiling paint colors may need to be lightened to compensate for this effect.

#57
Don't Reinvent the Wheel

To get a designer-selected color scheme for your home, find a designer fabric and look for its coordinated **paint collection**. Ralph Lauren, Laura Ashley, Alexander Julian, and other prominent designers offer professionally matched elements that can make decorating decisions nearly effortless. Ask your local retailer, or browse online to see coordinated lines of paints, fabrics, flooring, wallpaper, furniture, and accessories.

Count on contrast to crisp up a color scheme. White furniture against white walls could seem washed out; here, interesting furniture shapes are emphasized by the brilliant blue backdrop.

Chapter 6 Walls

As the largest surface in a home, walls play a major role in our décor. Whether presented as background or a focal point, walls are the container within which all other elements reside.

It follows that whatever is done to walls has enormous impact. A paint technique or wallcovering might look perfect on a small sample, yet the effect of applying it to four large walls might turn out a rousing success or something you'd just as soon forget.

While wall treatment types are many, the most common are **paint, wallpaper, wood, and other applied materials.**

PAINT is an easy choice. It's inexpensive, fairly simple to apply, and adds delicious color in any shade you desire. It can be rolled on as a single color, textured with faux and colorwashing techniques, or embellished with stenciling or borders. More elaborate paint techniques, including murals and *tromp l'oeil* ("fool the eye"), require an artistic eye and may call for the services of a professional decorative painter.

With any painting project, preparation is everything. Filling cracks, sanding, smoothing, and priming the walls usually takes far longer than applying the final coat, yet these steps are absolutely necessary for a beautiful finished project.

Besides paint color, you'll want to select an appropriate paint finish. Flat paints are traditional for walls, yet can be difficult to clean and may need periodic touching up with more paint. An eggshell or satin finish is easier to spot-clean with a sponge—a plus for homes with kids and pets.

WALLPAPER has many advantages. It adds pattern and interest to walls and is available in a multitude of themed designs, borders, and murals. Wallpaper manufacturers also offer a wide range of textures, grasscloths, and more, including designs that mimic a number of decorative paint effects, like spattering and colorwashing.

Wallpaper is a popular do-it-yourself project; however, it can be frustrating to install in a room with imperfect walls or lots of architectural features. If you're not up to the job, hiring a professional paperhanger may be a good solution.

WOOD walls include both **paneling** and applied **molding** details. Traditional, paneled walls render an elegant look (as shown on page 59 and 83), while beadboard panels (page 85 and 97) add a bit of country charm. Smooth wood panels (seen on page 94) can offer a contemporary feel.

Installing moldings on a wall is a project with high-yield results. Here are some ideas:

- Increase baseboard depth by nailing a narrow molding a few inches above the existing baseboard, then painting the new molding and the area below with the trim color.

- Add a chair rail molding applying one wall finish above and another below.

- Lower the perceived height of a ceiling by installing a strip of molding about 12 inches (30 cm) under the ceiling line. Paint the molding and everything above it with the ceiling color.

- Use a scroll saw to cut curves, waves, or triangle designs into standard lumber to use as a budget substitute for crown molding or chair rail.

Is that a beautiful vase of flowers? Yes, but it's created with paint, not blooms. The whimsical *tromp l'oeil* ("fool the eye") treatment opens a vista to imagined space beyond.

APPLIED MATERIALS include traditional and rustic treatments like these:

- Mirrors
- Tin panels
- Strips of bamboo, logs, or twigs
- Decoupaged maps, botanicals, or exotic papers
- Textured plaster walls

- Faux brick or stone
- Fabric panels and draperies
- Wall upholstery
- Sheets of copper or other metals
- Grasscloth matting materials

Walls

#58
Test and Modify

Try out any new wall treatment, paint, or faux technique on wallboard or poster board first. You'll avoid major wall disasters and have an opportunity to practice with the tools and materials, learning how to get the best effect for your project. Refine colors, tools, materials, and techniques, and keep testing until you're satisfied. It's better to work out the bugs ahead of time, before you've wasted half the weekend in false starts on your room's walls.

#59
Stamp It

Imitate wallpaper by applying repeating patterns to painted walls with stamps or stencils. Try taupe diamonds on an ivory wall or silver metallic scrolls on a deep gray wall. Random repeats offer a casual look. Alternatively, mark even gridlines or cut a square template out of cardboard for an evenly spaced repeat, then rubber stamp or stencil on your designs, using the grid or template to maintain alignment.

#60
Plaster Relief

Get an embossed look on a wall with stencils and spackle. Tape the stencil in place and use a putty knife to apply a thin layer of spackle or joint compound to the stencil. Carefully remove the stencil and leave the embossed area alone, or carve in some texture as it hardens. Let dry several days, then prime, paint, and decorate with metallic leaf or glazes. Finally, seal with two coats of polyurethane.

#61
Cap the Room with Crown Molding

Crown molding is the perfect finishing touch to bridge the transition from walls to ceiling. Designers generally specify 1 inch (2.5 cm) of molding height for every foot (31 cm) of ceiling height. Thus, a 9-foot (2.7 m) ceiling might have a 9-inch (23 cm) crown; however, you may want to size the formula down for smaller rooms and lower ceiling heights. In simpler rooms, get the look of crown molding without the expense by using lengths of flat lumber detailed with a few inexpensive stock moldings.

Wallpaper with a subtle pattern envelops a tiny space without intruding. Wall-mounted lamps and minimal window treatments help keep the room open and light.

Walls

#62
Stencil on a Motif

The appeal of stenciling is that it's a **fast and easy project** that requires few materials. A cut stencil, a bit of craft paint or interior wall paint, and a brush or sponge is just about all you'll need. If you can't locate the perfect stencil design, cut your own out of clear Mylar sheets, using a copy machine to reduce or enlarge a design traced from fabric or a pattern book. Find more tips from stencil supply sites on the Internet.

#63
Colorwashing Can Soften

Wiping diluted paint onto a wall with a dry brush or lint-free cloth is the essence of colorwashing. It's just about that easy. Research basic techniques before experimenting with color combinations and applications. This technique adds dimension to plain painted walls and is also recommended as a softening layer over stenciling and murals, enhancing them with a slightly aged appearance. Stains and glazes can also be colorwashed onto a wall.

#64
Go Geometric

Paint applied in geometric designs can **add subtle interest**. For example, tape off wide stripes, diamonds, or squares on a wall, like the pretty stripes on page 79. Get a neat tone-on-tone effect by filling some sections with flat paint and adjoining areas with the identical color in a satin or eggshell finish. For a more colorful treatment, do a faux finish or apply a palette of paint colors.

#65
Use the Good Stuff

The ceiling, often referred to as the fifth wall, is traditionally white. Instead of using inexpensive ceiling paint, however, paint your ceilings with a **good-quality wall paint**. This allows you to fine-tune the exact colors to coordinate with the rest of your room. While flat paint is the usual choice, a satin or eggshell finish can be applied on a ceiling in perfect condition. The added shine will boost light reflections within the room.

A flower-motif border accentuates a pretty arched ceiling and outlines the oversize arrangements of twigs in pottery jars.

Walls

#66
Faux Mural Solutions

Professionally painted murals are gorgeous but pricey. **Get a similar look** with scenes printed on mural wallpaper. Alternatively, order a set of large mural stencils to create an outdoor vista with paint. Some mural designs are also available in ceramic tile. Any of these can be applied directly to the wall, but for a removable treatment, apply them to a board attached to the wall with moldings.

#67
Architectural Molding

The area of wall under a chair rail is the perfect place for added **architectural interest**. As pictured on the opposite page, rectangles of molding are mitered, installed, and painted with the trim color. This is a project most homeowners can tackle, as it requires more time than money. Measure your walls for optimum placement of each section, taking care to work around vents and electrical outlets.

#68
Bring the Outdoors In

Faux clouds can open up a child's room, powder room, entryway, hall, or porch. (You'll find techniques in a faux painting book and on the Internet.) This look can be applied to walls as well as smaller ceilings, or within a small oval section in the center of a larger ceiling. Practice first on a board to perfect the paint colors and techniques.

Lively vines and flowers scroll onto the wall between lavishly striped drapery panels, effectively replacing artwork and accessories.

Looking for Wall Tips on the Internet

- www.paintquality.com/colorchart/index.html
- www.wallcoverings.org
- www.hometime.com/Howto/projects/paint.htm

Chapter 7

Window Treatments

Windows are the eyes and ears of a house. They allow us to see and hear nature and the neighborhood just outside the glass. Open them, and they beckon summer breezes. Close them, and they keep out the harsh chill of winter. We stand at them to wave children off to school and sit by them to read or work.

With the light and energy windows bring to a home, it's a shame to cover them up—yet few of us want to live in a fishbowl, especially at night. As darkness falls, we cherish our privacy and feel cozier when shades are pulled or curtains drawn. This illustrates the basic need for window treatments to provide **privacy**.

Once day breaks, however, we love seeing the sunlight stretch into our rooms, brightening corners and supplying warmth. As much as we welcome the sun, however, we also need to be aware of its power. Fabrics, rugs—indeed, nearly anything that has color (like artwork or wood)—will fade, lose, or change color under regular exposure to the sun's rays.

Light control is, therefore, the second important function of window treatments. It makes sense, then, to choose window treatments that address these two core issues. Soft shades and draperies work well when closed, but shutters and blinds may be better choices for privacy and light control. Tilt the movable slats of blinds up to shield interiors from direct sunlight, then raise the blinds altogether after the sun peaks

high overhead and no longer threatens to fade our furnishings.

Whether your interiors call for the clean lines of plantation shutters, the textured simplicity of bamboo blinds, or the softness of fabric panels, **style**—the third property of window treatments—is the element that contributes a certain look to an interior.

Fabric on windows can be as small as a valance or as elaborate as a full set of draperies. To get the benefit of fabric on a budget, consider installing nonfunctioning stationary panels flanking each window, like the navy plaid shown on the opposite page. Because the panels are each made from only one or two widths of fabric, they are often less expensive than draperies made to cover the full width of the glass.

Another option for windows is to improvise a **no-sew swagged treatment**. These are fashioned from a long length of fabric hooked into place at the center of the window and at each corner. Although special hardware is available for this do-it-yourself project, any piece of hardware with a large ring or elbow—including towel rings, large drawer pulls, twig wreaths, plant holders, drapery tie-back hardware, and more—might be employed. Secure your fabric creations with knots, wire, pipe cleaners, wire ties, clothespins, or binder clips.

Drapery rods with clip rings also facilitate easy no-sew treatments. Attach the rings to any

White sheers soften the expanse of glass while navy plaid drapery panels bracket the windows with color.

length of fabric that roughly fits your window size. Flat sheets, tablecloths, widths of fabric, lace, or even lightweight blankets and quilts are all possibilities. Hem the edges (sew or use fabric glue), or simply tuck raw edges underneath and puddle the drape onto the floor.

Whether you opt for fabric panels, a no-sew treatment, or professionally made draperies, **consider installing your curtain rods before making or ordering window treatments**. With the hardware in place, your measurements can be exact, and the treatments are more likely to fit perfectly.

Finally, do consider every window treatment's **operation**, especially in areas with high windows, arched glass, French doors, or bay windows, as all of these require specialized solutions. Swing-arm rods, remote-control blinds, arched shades, and custom coverings are just a few of the possibilities.

Framing your windows with layers that add **privacy, light control, style, and function** will highlight them and help complete your design ideas.

Window Treatments

#69
Stand Back before Ordering

Before ordering patterned draperies, be sure to view a **full-length panel of the fabric** from a distance of 10 feet (3 m) or more. This lets you preview the pattern, color, and fabric as it will appear in the finished drape. Large patterns sometimes disappear into the fabric folds, while smaller repeats can melt into an entirely different look. This may be fine, but you want to know so you can make any adjustments before ordering.

#70
Kiss or Puddle Hems for Drama

Drapes that don't touch the floor can look a bit off-kilter. It's more elegant to **install drapes so hems kiss the floor** (see page 66). Most sumptuous of all is a puddled hem. Add an extra 2 to 8 inches (5 to 20 cm) to a drape's length for a mild puddle effect, and more if you want even more drama. The extra length also keeps fabric panels from lifting too high off the floor when tied back.

Long draperies puddle softly on the floor while bringing color to the room and framing the view. Layered underneath are wood blinds to control sunlight and privacy.

#71
Cut Up a Bamboo Blind

Inexpensive matchstick or bamboo blinds can be cut and used for an effective textured valance. Cut off 24-inch (31 cm) sections, being sure to tie off and glue the connecting threads so the blind won't unravel. Attach the top edge to a narrow board hung over the window. Roll up a few inches of the bottom "hem." Finish by attaching a folded length of cording, fabric strips, or ribbon to the top board and knotting it under the rolled hem (see an example on page 117) to hold it in place.

#72
Try an Unusual Valance

Need a **window valance on a budget**? Want to try something different? These treatments may be just the ticket. Though they may not last forever, they can add whimsy and unique style to a room.

- Thread baskets onto a curtain rod as a three-dimensional valance; fill the end baskets with trailing ivy, if desired.

- Attach a decorative metal grille or scrollwork piece to the wall above the window frame.

- String beads or chandelier crystals on lengths of sheer ribbon tied to a rod.

- Use raffia to tie vintage kitchen utensils to a rod.

- Fold heavy decorative paper into wide horizontal pleats so it looks like a Roman shade, punch a few lengths of twine through all layers, and suspend in a small window.

- Swag colorful vintage tablecloths along a rod, gathering them up every 2 feet (61 cm) or so to tie in place with cording.

Window Treatments

#73
Contrast Decorative Hardware

Decide if **drapery hardware** should be unobtrusive (as in the photo here and on page 14) or a noticeable accent. Drapery poles, brackets, and hardware that **match** the wall or trim color will practically disappear. However, they will **stand out** if they sport a contrasting color, such as black iron rods against a white wall (see examples on page 61 and 66). You might also paint or faux-finish rods to match or accent the wall color.

#74
Pillowcase Your Drapery Panels

Get two looks from your drapery panels by lining them with a contrasting fabric. Ask for this "pillowcase-style" treatment when ordering custom flat-panel or rod-top drapes. Try a toile lined with white damask or a yellow floral backed with a soft green check. Turn the panels to the opposite side for a new look for summer and winter. White interlining between the layers should prevent the contrasting fabric from showing through.

#75
Have Your Sheers and Privacy, Too

If you love the look of sheers but need more **privacy** than they provide, look for styles with embroidery or patterning. Alternatively, use two layers of sheer fabric, a sheer over an opaque fabric, or sheer bands sewn into an opaque panel. For maximum privacy, hang sheers over a roller shade, shutters, or an opaque café curtain.

#76
Creative Rods Add to a Theme

Support a themed room by **replacing traditional drapery rods** with an unusual alternative. Narrow bamboo poles, sturdy dowels, closet poles, copper or plastic piping, and fun theme elements, such as golf clubs, hockey sticks, and tree branches, are whimsical ways to hold up window treatments with style. These can go a long way toward boosting the personality of a room.

Flat, two-sided drapery panels swag casually from wood rods. Folding back the top and side edges reveals the coordinated lining that effectively acts as a border detail.

Window Treatments

#77
Borders for Punch

Treat plain drapery panels to decorating detail **by adding a border** or band of contrasting fabric during a drapery panel's fabrication. Alternatively, sew or glue a ribbon border to the top, bottom, or sides of a finished panel. Try a navy border on plain white curtains or a yellow border, like the one shown on page 102. Other border treatments include fringe, tassels, and trims of beads or crystals.

#78
Swing-Arm Style

Swing-arm rods offer convenience for many applications. Hanging fabric panels on this hardware allows draperies to open quickly, facilitating easy access to a window or door. Swing-arm rods also are a good solution for tight spaces where a window is very close to a wall, but are best used where space allows them to open and close without interfering with furniture or other room features.

#79
Tension Rods
Solve Move-in Blues

Take advantage of inexpensive metal tension rods to fashion **temporary window treatments** in a new home. Fit the rod into your window frame, then drape a temporary covering that's cut or folded to size. The drape should be the height of the window glass plus at least 24 inches (61 cm) to loop over the rod. Fold it around the rod a few times to make a daytime "valance" and pull down to full length for privacy at night. Here are some ideas:

- Sheeting cut to fit window widths
- Flat curtain panels from your old house, folded to fit the width of the window (lightweight sheers work best here)
- Kraft paper (long rolls of brown paper) cut to fit your windows
- Towels or lightweight blankets folded to fit
- Table runners or tablecloths
- Inexpensive fabric (burlap, felt, muslin)

Sumptuous silk stripes pull together all the colors in the room. The wall tone is matched in the border sewn onto the drapery hem.

Looking for Window Treatments on the Internet
- www.smithandnoble.com
- www.ruedefrance.com
- www.bedbathandbeyond.com

Chapter 8
Living Rooms

Ask a dozen homeowners how they use their living room and you're likely to get a dozen different answers. The living room, after all, is either the favorite gathering spot or the most overlooked room in the house.

Large homes may include a family room, a den, and a media room that replace many of the functions of a traditional living room. Except for formal entertaining, those living rooms may see little service.

Yet, in a smaller home the living room may be one area that's large enough to accommodate family activities and entertaining. It's a multi-purpose space that's an integral part of daily life.

Decorating a living room, therefore, must be a uniquely personal expression of your particular lifestyle. The furniture should correspond to the way you use the room. Is the room used mainly for entertaining? You might plan for lots of

chairs and sofas. Is it used for nightly reading or television? Choose comfortable seating and adequate reading lamps, arranged in front of an entertainment center or fireplace. Is the space used to practice music or pay bills? Arrange for furnishings to accommodate those specific activities.

The **checklist** on the following page will help you determine what might work best for your space.

Your answers should narrow your focus and provide preliminary goals for a living room decorating plan. They may also eliminate choices, freeing you to concentrate on the most appropriate options. After all, when the styles you'd like to consider include Country Swedish and French, that means you won't need to look at contemporary or retro furnishings.

Whenever you're considering a purchase for the living room—or any room—compare the item's characteristics with the your list of goals for the space. **Does it match or clash?** Thoughtfully determining if a piece is **appropriate to the goals of style and function** can help decide which elements to include and which to decline.

A serene living room offers classic solutions for small spaces: a light color palette, glass-topped table, neat symmetry, unobtrusive window treatments, and an uncluttered style.

Here's a list of items to consider when decorating a living room.

- The dimensions of my living room are:

  _____ x _____

- The main focal point of the room is:

  _____

- I/we entertain guests _____ times a month/year

- I we would like seating for (how many people)

  _____ in the living room

- I/we plan to use the room for an hour or more

  about _____ times a week

- I/we need space for these activities in the living room:

  – Reading

  – Watching TV or movies

  – Listening to or playing music

  – Playing games

  – Paying bills

  – Computer activities

  – Office work

  – Entertaining friends

  – Hobbies

  _ Displaying collections

  – Other: _____

(Circle all that apply)

- I prefer an overall style that is:

  Formal / Informal / Casual

- In my ideal living room my favorite place to sit would be:

  comfy upholstered chair / leather chair /

  wicker chair / French side chair / recliner

- I prefer furnishings that are:

  Traditional / Contemporary / Eclectic / Rustic/

  Antique / New / Dramatic / of a specific style

  (French, Italian, Asian, etc.)

  _____

- I prefer colors that are:

  Warm / Cool / Neutral / White / Dramatic /

  Restful / Cozy / Pale / Deep / Bright / Natural

- I prefer wood tones that are:

  Light / Medium / Dark / Painted

- I prefer flooring that is:

  Hardwood / Tile / Carpeting / Stone /

  Laminate / Sisal

- I prefer area rugs that are:

  Oriental / Seagrass / Floral / Contemporary /

  Abstract / Needlepoint / Geometric / Plain

- I prefer window treatments that include:

  Draperies / Sheers / Bamboo Shades / Metal

  Blinds / Wood Blinds / Shutters / Soft Shades

- I prefer accessories that are:

  Traditional / Contemporary / Rustic /

  Country / Exotic / Global / Themed / Artistic

- I like accents that are:

  Silver / Gold / Glass / Steel / Metallic / Wood /

  Stone / Antique / Weathered / Ceramic / Porcelain

- The one thing I really want in this room is:

  _____

- The one thing I don't want in this room is:

  _____

- Styles I'm considering include:

  _____

- Styles I don't care for include:

  _____

This charming room successfully breaks many so-called living room rules in featuring a tall coffee table, a black floor, no window treatments, and few accessories.

Living Rooms

#80
Avoid Blocking Natural Pathways

Examine your room's layout and **determine what normal walkways exist**. These include direct routes between a door and a window, to a closet, or to any other feature of the room, such as a fireplace. Draw these pathways on your floorplan and, whenever possible, avoid placing furniture where it might interrupt the traffic flow.

#81
Create Mirror Magic

Large mirrors are a classic in a living or dining room and can visually increase the apparent size of a space. Mirrors placed where they reflect an outdoor view are especially attractive. Look for mirrors with elegant beveled edges, styles with interesting shapes (arched, round, oval, or square), or hang a collection of mirrors together for lots of sparkle.

#82
Watch the Legs

Give your room the leg test. **Do all of the furnishings have exposed legs**? This can sometimes make a living room seem like a forest of sticks. What can you do? Try adding one skirted table. Solid furnishings such as trunks, chests, and cabinets also add a smoother line to the room. Finally, chairs and sofas with skirts that drop to the floor offer a way to disguise legs.

#83
Do Something Different for a Coffee Table

Ramp up a living room's style by **reinventing the coffee table**. Place it 12 to 16 inches (31 to 41 cm) in front of the couch—any closer will be too cramped and any farther away will be unusable. Here are some options:

- A set of four square ottomans
- A tall tea table (see photo opposite)
- An antique trunk
- A pair of tray tables
- A stack of wood boxes or vintage suitcases
- A tiled tabletop on metal legs
- Three wooden cubes covered with grasscloth
- A vintage wood or padded bench
- An old dining table with its legs cut down
- A sturdy concrete garden ornament topped with glass

Living Rooms

#84

Set the Conversation Area

When arranging furniture, place the largest pieces first, then the smaller items. Conversation areas placed to take advantage of the room's focal point are most successful when furniture is arranged to fit inside a circle or square that's **8 to 14 feet** (2.4 to 4.3 m) across.

#85

Don't Block the View

Choose **low pieces of furniture when placing them in front of a window** with views to the outside or in a room that looks into an adjoining space. Chaises, benches, ottomans, and backless settees offer extra seating without blocking sightlines. The extended view can also help visually enlarge a room.

#86

Decorate Empty Corners

Jazz up an empty corner in a room by filling it with something interesting. A large plant, either real or artificial, is a common choice, but many other possibilities can be explored:

- A chair and ottoman angled into a corner
- A corner cupboard or armoire
- An angled desk or game table
- A folding screen
- A tall plant stand with one beautiful fern
- A round pedestal or skirted table
- Artwork on an easel
- A decorative object (sculpture, pottery) on a column

Furniture pulled into a conversational grouping can leave corners bare. The solution in this room is to decorate those spaces with plants and art.

#87
Bring Furniture to the Center

Conversation areas **arranged in the center of the living room** involve a few practical considerations to work out. How will you plug in the lamp that's now far from the nearest outlet? Ask an electrician about installing floor outlets under the furniture. If that's not possible, then overhead recessed or track lighting is another option.

Living Rooms

Smaller pieces of furniture, such as side tables, benches, ottomans, and desks, offer function and flexibility, and they permit easy rearrangement to suit changing needs.

#88
Furniture Smart for Moving

Do you move frequently? **Smaller furnishings** can be a better choice for a nomadic lifestyle. They'll generally be easier to lift, fit through doorways, and settle into new digs without hassle. A pair of loveseats (rather than a giant sofa) can be placed together or separately. Small chests are versatile enough to use in any room, and occasional items like side tables, chairs, and bookshelves can also give flexible service in a variety of locations.

#89
Sofa Bed Style

Are you thinking about buying a futon or a sofa bed? These items of furniture can be useful for overnight guests. However, be aware that they will rarely be as comfortable to sit on as a regular sofa. Determine if it's worth compromising your **daily enjoyment of a sofa** for infrequent use as a bed. If not, perhaps a self-inflating air mattress is a solution for guests until your home includes a full-fledged guest room.

Twin tables can be pushed together or apart and include plenty of surface area for accessory display

#90
Protect Your Upholstered Furniture

Fading and stains are two risks for upholstered furnishings. **Preempt damage from fading** by installing window tinting or using light-controlling window treatments on sunny days. As for stains, many furniture manufacturers label furniture with **cleaning codes**. Read those instructions and put together a small kit with recommended stain-removing solutions and clean rags. Also, stash a few small towels under seat cushions to help quickly contain spills.

#91
Go Up, Up, Up

As a public space, a living room can have a grander feel than the rest of a home. Emphasize this quality by using elements that **add height to the room**. Hang draperies from floor to ceiling. Put up a tall mirror or stack a group of paintings one over another to accentuate a vertical line. Tall bookshelves, striped wall treatments, and large armoires are other ways to go up in a living room.

Chapter 9
Dining Rooms

The dining room holds a warm spot in many a heart. As the room that hosts family holidays and celebrations, it's a space where fond memories are made and cherished.

The requirements for a dining room are basic: a table, some chairs, display space, and perhaps some storage. Yet these elements can be combined in endless variety to create a beautiful and functional room.

Dining tables last a lifetime and beyond, so whether you want a vintage piece that comes with patina and unspoken history or a brand-new table with a smooth, shiny surface, you're likely to make this purchase only once. It makes sense, then, to adopt a dining table that speaks to you.

If you haven't yet found your "perfect" dining room furnishings, it's fairly easy to make do. Paint the walls a delicious color to take the focus off the furnishings. Cover a makeshift plywood table with felt (for softness) and a floor-length tablecloth. Bring in some benches or mismatched flea market chairs that have been finished or slipcovered alike. You'll have a useful dining space as you continue the quest for your perfect table and chairs.

When choosing a table, consider the table's dimensions within your dining space. Next, determine how many chairs and placemats might fit at a table, and note whether there's room for a flower arrangement or centerpiece. In addition, consider the expansion options the table offers. Whenever possible, try out a table with the chairs you plan to use with it.

Avoid tables that wobble or have supports that interfere with chairs or feet. Steer clear of styles too narrow for a centerpiece or that include a deep apron that bumps your knees as you pull a chair in close.

Do look for beautifully finished tabletop surfaces and a design that expands and contracts for entertaining large or small groups. (See more about tables in tips #93, #94, and #96.)

Dining room chairs offer multiple options as well (see tips #92, #97, #99, and #102). You'll want to try chairs for both comfort and their suitability with your table. Remember, you'll be sitting in these chairs for many hours over the years, so comfort is vital.

Are chairs light enough to move effortlessly, yet solid enough to withstand normal use? Are the chair backs contoured or straight? Do the arms slide easily under the table's edge? Will fully upholstered chairs require frequent upkeep and reupholstering? Should you consider a chair style with removable seats that can be easily recovered by stapling on a new fabric? All of these questions should factor into a purchasing decision—yet **true love endures**, so aim most of all for pieces you genuinely adore.

Color a dining room to harmonize with both dinnerware and adjoining room spaces. Because many dining areas are most often used in the evening, a dark wall color can lend richness and warmth, while pale tones serve to surround a dining room in serenity. What's your preference?

Decorate your dining room thoughtfully. Give yourself time to find that "just-right" table, the perfect mix of chairs, and an attractive sideboard. Choose colors and fabrics to blend with your home and frame precious family meals. If you can do all that, your dining room will be a smashing success.

The objects displayed on this sideboard resonate with the images seen in the oil painting.

Dining Rooms

#92
Don't Fight the Food

While dining room chair upholstery may be fruited or flowered, bright or bold, you'll enjoy added flexibility when you **keep it understated**. Plain or subtly patterned upholstery won't compete with your china, food, or centerpieces and may allow more freedom to create colorful holiday table settings. Bring in seasonal style with slipcovers, perhaps switching to luxurious velvet for winter or a crisp organdy sheer for summer.

#93
Shape Matters

What kind of dining table do you prefer? Rectangular tables are traditional favorites and often include leaves that extend the table for more guests. Round tables are prized for facilitating warm conversation. Some models extend into long ovals to accommodate more guests. Square and octagonal tables offer similar benefits. Can't decide? **Consider your room's layout**—whether it might accommodate one shape better than another.

#94
The Skinny on Glass Tables

Glass tables have a disappearing **see-through style** that fits well in many homes. The drawback to glass is its inflexibility in adapting to different size gatherings. If you consistently entertain six for dinner, a nonexpanding glass table might be just right. However, if you like cozy dinners for four one week and a sit-down supper for twelve the next, look for a dining table that expands and contracts easily.

#95
Double Your Dining Pleasure

Stash an extra table in a closet or basement to use as a second dining table when entertaining large groups. Buy a table with folding legs, or fashion your own inexpensive table with a circle of plywood set on a stable base. Set your temporary table in a foyer, family room, or porch. Covered with a layer of soft quilting or felt and a beautiful floor-length tablecloth, no one will know there is unfinished wood underneath.

Classic glass sits atop a fluted pedestal base for see-through dining. Sparkling chandelier pendants and a rock crystal centerpiece provide textural contrast to the sheen of silk draperies and the subtly striped walls.

The blue, gold, and ivory color scheme repeats the hues found in the patterned rug. The same colors appear in the table setting, chandelier, and artwork.

Dining Rooms

#96
Cool It Off with Stone

Glass, stone, marble, and tile tabletops offer a smooth, **cool surface for dining** that's just right for a contemporary interior or a home located in a tropical clime. However, stone surfaces may feel cold and uninviting during the chilly months of winter. When the temperature drops, use table pads or a quilted liner under a tablecloth. Consider choosing a wood table instead if you prefer a warmer feel.

#97
Fancy It Up with Monograms

Detail plain dining chair slipcovers with refined style by having the backs embroidered in a large monogram or design motif. For a touch of whimsy, each chair might be monogrammed differently with a name, number, or word. A thread that matches the fabric offers a tone-on-tone look, while a contrasting thread color might relate to the room's color scheme.

#98
Get Out the China

Even if you use your best dishes just a few days a year, they needn't stay under wraps the rest of the time. **Show off pretty plates** as decorations in your dining room. Arranging them in a china cabinet is the traditional option, but china can also be set upright in plate holders on a sideboard, placed on wall-hung plate racks, or displayed along a plate rail near the ceiling.

Looking for Monogramming on the Internet
- www.graciousstyle.com
- www.monogrammedlinenshop.com
- www.givingtreeonline.com

Dining Rooms

#99
Stand Back for Chair Backs

Many times, the first thing you see in a dining room is the backs of the chairs. Are they attractive or boring? **Dress up chair backs with details** that catch the eye. Slip on headrest covers of pretty fabric, or drape a swirl of sheer fabric over a chair and catch it in a knot of raffia. Consider making slipcovers with box pleats, monograms, ties, buttons, or tabs to decorate the chair backs.

#100
Tailor a Tablecloth

Give any dining table a new lease on life by **draping it in a tablecloth**. Whether your choice is a ready-made short cloth, a custom-made to-the-floor style, or an elegant sheer, the color and fabric will lend softness and personality to the room. Want a more tailored look? Try styles with crisp box pleats held closed with flat, buttoned tabs.

#101
Level the Seating Field

Dining room chairs—no matter how diverse or creatively placed—should have one thing in common: the **seats should all be the same height**. If you have a collection of mismatched chairs, alter the seat heights by adding cushions (thin or thick) to shorter chairs. Nailing button feet to the legs can also add more height. These modifications will make sure everyone feels part of the group and no one gets stuck in a chair that's too short.

#102
Nix the Matching Chairs

Instead of a perfectly matched set of eight dining chairs, have some fun! **Mix, match, paint, or slipcover chairs** for a look that's uniquely yours. Here are other ideas for dining chair options:

- Use a loveseat or settee on one side of the table.

- Replace two chairs with a bench or large ottoman.

- Mix two styles of chairs with alternating high and low backs.

- Pair fully upholstered chairs with traditional wood chairs.

- Paint inexpensive chairs all white or all black; for a fun, casual look, paint each a different color.

Boost the style of slipcovers by adding detail where it counts. Seen from an adjoining room, the back pleats on these chairs add interest to the view.

Chapter 10

Bedrooms

If there's one room that's totally your own, it's the master bedroom. This is where you probably spend the majority of your time at home—most of that alone or with a partner. Because others view this room only momentarily, it's yours to decorate in any way you desire.

One of the first words that comes to mind regarding a master bedroom is *retreat*—a room where we can shut out some of the cares and routine of daily life and surround ourselves with elements that bring us comfort and serenity.

Just because a room is **serene**, however, doesn't mean it must be boring. Your perfect bedroom could be a minimal contemporary space with straight lines and dramatic accessories. It might be a floral garden retreat brimming with pretty color, or a room done in black and white toile with a French flair.

Can't decide? Consider what you'd **most like to see** when you open your eyes every morning. Can you use the colors you saw at a romantic inn? Are you fond of a certain motif or theme? Can your collections be the inspiration for a distinctive room? Do you own a piece of art you want to highlight? Any of these can be the springboard for a refreshingly distinctive bedroom.

Think carefully about furniture in **smaller bedrooms**, where you'll often need to be creative with the arrangement. For example, place a bed in front of a window (see page 13), angled into a corner (see page 142), or at the end of a tiny space (see page 55).

Ideally, a bedroom is large enough to accommodate more than just a bed. A **cozy reading area** with comfortable seating is a must—perhaps with a chaise, upholstered chair, or loveseat. Bedrooms may also have room for an armoire, bookshelves, or a writing desk.

Design features into your room that **solve particular challenges**. Need more storage? Replace a tiny bedside table with a full-size chest of drawers. Need more lighting? Install recessed fixtures, operated by convenient wall switches, over the bed. Need total darkness at night? Look for light-blocking window shades or blackout drapery linings. Tired of walking on cold, bare floors? Find an area rug, or have a carpet remnant bound to your size specifications.

Headboards are a mainstay of bedroom décor. If you're just starting out, however, you may have only purchased a mattress set and haven't found a headboard that fits your style.

Get just the size and shape you want by making your own headboard. This is an easy do-it-yourself project (see tip #103). If you'd like the headboard feel without the headboard look, try one of these options on the wall behind the bed:

- A vintage **window** or **door** hung behind the bed

- **Gates**, fence sections, or fancy iron scrollwork

- A **mirror** flanked by a pair of old shutters

- A large **picture frame** with a padded interior section where the art used to be

- A large **folding screen** attached flat to the wall

- An **artist's canvas** that you've painted in blocks of color

- Fabric **draperies** suspended on a rod

- A **tapestry** or rug hung on the wall

- A checkerboard of mirror **tiles**

- A rustic **twig headboard** (see page 13)

With all of these ideas about sleeping spaces and retreats, you're probably feeling more relaxed already. That's the power of a bedroom.

Black and white toile shines in this room next to
fresh white for a touch of class at bedtime.

These coordinated fabrics are repeated several times within the room and illustrate the harmonious result of basing a color scheme on fabric.

Bedrooms

#103
Add Height with Headboards

A headboard should be tall enough to be seen **above the pillow shams.** **Upholstered headboards** can be custom made, yet it's fairly simple and quite inexpensive to make your own. Cover a shaped wood backing with a layer of foam, batting, and white sheeting. Once you have secured all this with staples on the back of the board, stretch designer fabric over it as the final layer.

#104
Layer on a Bedskirt

Traditional rooms often employ a bedskirt to conceal the metal bed frame. While gathered styles predominated in the past, newer looks feature crisply tailored box pleats or simple flat panels. Custom bedskirts can be sewn with two back-to-back fabrics so the skirt will **reverse,** offering two distinct looks. Some contemporary beds may not need a skirt at all; consider opting for a **quilted box spring cover** instead.

#105
Choose Piles of Pillows or Just a Few

Many people adore decorative bed pillows like the ones shown here and on page 26. If this is your style, consider **how many pillows you really want** so bedmaking won't become a chore. Perhaps you prefer a minimalist style. In that case, try long bolsters and pillow stacking (one on top of another) for a simpler look (see page 91). Hide rumpled sleeping pillows in a nearby closet or chest.

#106
Change Comforters Seasonally

Decorate your bed for seasonal weather changes by alternating comforters and pillows at least twice a year. A soft cotton matelassé bed coverlet with cool white pillows is a perfect summer look. Sheer overlays—much like a tablecloth for your bed—are another pretty, romantic look for warm months. In cooler weather, switch to a cozy down comforter with a suitably warm-looking duvet cover.

A lovely writing desk positioned at the foot of the bed offers a secluded spot for a cup of tea and a place to catch up on thank-you notes.

Bedrooms

#107
Expand Bedside Tables

A little nightstand might be perfect for a single bed, yet larger beds need a more substantial look. Get it by placing a chest of drawers, desk, pedestal table, or skirted table next to the bed. These **larger furnishings are more in scale** with queen and king beds and allow more tabletop display area for lamps, books, and accessories.

#108
Double Up on Sheets

It's easy to decorate a room around a distinct bedding pattern, but plan ahead for wear and tear by purchasing **two complete sets of sheets** rather than just one. Alternate sets to extend their useful life, making your room décor last longer. Several sets of pillowcases kept crisply ironed will allow you the luxury of changing them every few days to freshen your bed.

#109
Furnish the Space at the End of the Bed

From narrow benches to a full-size loveseat, the end of the bed is a perfect place for useful furnishings. **Try a desk, a pair of upholstered chairs**, a large ottoman, trunk, or chest. As a bonus, when you use these furnishings to read, sit, or work, you'll be able to enjoy your gorgeous bedroom even more often.

#110
Slipcover a Headboard

Almost any headboard can be **slipcovered for a new look** when you move or redecorate a bedroom. Custom make a fitted cover, or simply attach ribbon ties to a flat fabric panel and fold it over an existing headboard. This is a wonderful way to impart a seasonal touch to your bedroom. Try velvet, damask, or tapestry in the winter and floral fabrics, embroidered sheers, or cool linen in the summer.

Bedrooms

#111
Cross-Link Colors within a Suite

Visually link a master bedroom with an attached sitting room or master bath by continuing the color scheme throughout the space. You could feature terra-cotta walls with accents of blue in the bedroom, then reverse the colors to use blue in the bathroom with accessories of terra-cotta. **Coordinated fabric** collections (like the ones shown on pages 20-22) are another choice for this technique.

#112
Top a Table with Mirror

Topping a table's surface with **glass or mirror** adds extra sparkle to a room. This is a wonderful finishing touch for a homemade round, square, or rectangular table. Make the table to the size you desire from wood and sturdy legs, then cover it with a tablecloth before topping with a sheet of mirror.

#113
Add a Faux Canopy

Even if you don't have a four-poster bed, you can **give a romantic touch to your bed with fabric**. Invent the illusion of a canopy by hanging large metal rings from the ceiling, each positioned above one corner of the bed. Drape yards of sheer fabric up and over each ring for the four-poster look at a fraction of the cost. Puddle the ends of the fabric onto the floor for even more drama.

#114
Supersize a Closet

Every closet in the house will benefit from installing a well-planned **closet system**. Custom designed or ready-made, models are available to accommodate every budget. Look for features like specialty drawers for jewelry, Plexiglas doors to help keep clothes dust free, and pull-out tie racks. Browse online for ideas, or call a professional to design a closet interior that will **maximize your closet space**.

Create your own view with art. Here, a large landscape painting stands in for a window and gives the impression of an outdoor vista.

Chapter 11 Baths

From tiny powder rooms to luxuriously appointed master suites, bathrooms today are being designed for **style** as much as **function**. The bathroom is found in an endless variety of sizes, shapes, and degrees of formality—yet it frequently starts out as little more than a plain vanilla box, ready for the special touches that give it personality.

With a large remodeling budget, anyone can have a bathroom fit for a princess or at least a movie star. Marble floors, glass tile, whirlpool tubs, computerized shower modules, and custom cabinetry are just a few of the extravagant alternatives that inspire homeowners to create private sanctuaries for personal pampering.

Smaller budgets might not include replacing the tub or expanding the room, but even a less elaborate makeover with **paint**, **wallpaper**, **flooring**, **and lighting** can offer major rewards with minimal disruption and minor expense.

The most budget-friendly makeover project is **paint**. Although preparation can be labor-intensive, paint offers do-it-yourself fix-up with luscious color.

Wallpaper is another alternative to fill rooms with color and pattern. Because wall surfaces in a bathroom are often limited (with mirrors, doors, windows, and tile taking up a good portion of the wall area), wallpaper may be an affordable option. Wallpaper, however, is best suited to bathrooms that are not exposed to steamy showers every day.

This chapter includes ideas on reworking existing bathrooms on a budget. Note, however, that some of the most important tips are also the most frugal: fastidious cleaning, decluttering,

and repairing eyesores such as stained grout and chipped paint. Periodically purge vanity paraphernalia so whatever is no longer useful won't take up valuable bathroom real estate. Covered boxes, baskets, and other decorative containers can corral the jumble of items often found on bath counters. Place groups of similar objects, like perfume bottles or washcloths, on **trays** or in **baskets** for a neater look.

Once these tasks are complete, move on to fresh ideas and decorating solutions:

- Rework a wall of **mirror** from the 1960s by giving it a makeover (see tips #116 and #121).

- Install new **light fixtures** (see tip #117).

- Add **furniture** to a bathroom when space permits. A chest or armoire provides useful storage. A small bench or chair offers a handy place to sit while drying your hair or applying makeup.

- Replacing an outdated vanity with a **pedestal sink** (see tip #115) will make a huge impact in a cramped bathroom; be warned, however, that you'll probably need to renew the flooring as well.

Still too much work? Simply switching to brand-new **towels**, **rugs**, **shower curtains**, **and window treatments** can revive a tired-looking bath in a single afternoon. Piles of new towels add softness and color. Stack or hang them in new and unusual ways (see tip #126). Collect them in all white, a mix of pastels, or an array of bright accent colors. Their soft luxury may make you feel like a celebrity in your own private oasis.

Turn a small bathroom into a jewel box. The same print on the walls and window drapery unites the space as graceful lines curve around the niche, mirror, vanity, sink, and faucets.

Baths

#115
Make Way for Pedestals

Tiny bathrooms can often be improved by removing space-hogging vanities and replacing them with **sleek pedestal sinks**. The newly empty floor area will immediately make the room feel larger. Some pedestal sinks include a useful flat rim area to hold soap or a glass. Additional shelving, a linen closet, or freestanding furniture can replace lost vanity storage.

#116
Do Something Unexpected with Mirrors

Hang a round, oval, square, or tall mirror in place of that predictable rectangle. Alternatively, simply hang a large framed mirror over an existing mirrored wall, using long wires securely attached to the ceiling or wall (where they won't interfere with the existing mirror). Disguise the wires with ribbon or cording. Have a big blank wall? Fill it with a **collection of framed mirrors** for a new look.

#117
Update Tired Light Fixtures

Replace unimaginative light fixtures with something new and fresh. Look for a style to complement your room. Change the lighting altogether by hiring an electrician to add wall boxes for **a pair of attractive sconces** placed at eye level on either side of the mirror. They'll offer pleasant light and good looks.

#118
Bring In Fabric

Fabric can make a world of difference in a room filled with hard surfaces. Avoid the cold look of a plastic shower curtain by layering a fabric drapery over it for pattern and color. Although ready-made fabric curtains are available, it's simple to **make your own** from decorator fabric or a sheet, hemming it a few inches larger than the measurements of the plastic liner. Finish the top with buttonholes, tabs, ties, or grommets.

The warmth of wood offsets the cold look of porcelain fixtures. Protect wood surfaces with several coats of polyurethane and dry water spills immediately.

Baths

#119
Look for More Space

Tiny bathrooms need every inch of space, so seize every opportunity for storage. Here are some ideas:

- Attach a narrow shelf high on the wall for an out-of-the-way display space for collectibles.

- Install wall-hung shelf units.

- Set out baskets or vintage boxes to hold cosmetics or display towels.

- Maximize storage in a linen closet by adding additional shelves, roll-out drawers, shelf labels, and lighting.

#120
Expand with Diagonals

Visually expand a room by using a **diagonal pattern on the floor**. The floor in this room was painted white, then overlaid with a grid of lavender squares set on the diagonal. The longer lines of the diamond shapes draw your eye into the room and make the floor appear wider. This is a wonderful technique to use in any room that feels confined.

#121
Frame a Wall of Mirror

Take a wall-to-wall vanity mirror to the next level by **framing the perimeter with a beautiful picture frame molding**. Choose a traditional stained molding, a colorful painted style, or a sleek fluted look that's been metal-leafed. Finish the back of the molding as well, as it will be reflected in the mirror image. Miter the corners or use straight cuts paired with corner block rosettes. Nail the frame to the wall or use silicone caulk to attach the frame directly to the mirror.

#122
Add Innovative Storage

Many objects intended for use in another room can be adapted for unusual bathroom storage. Have a tiny unused corner? A **tall kitchen pot rack**—a narrow metal triangular tower about 5 feet (1.5 m) high—can hold hand towels, plants, or baskets of soaps. Do you have a small **wine rack** you like? Bring it into the bathroom and fill the spaces with rolled towels. Milk crates, sap buckets, and laundry baskets are more options.

Looking for Tile on the Internet

- www.annsackstile.com
- www.walkerzanger.com
- interiordec.about.com

  Search for "Tile"

In a color scheme inspired by collectible pitchers, rich lavender combines with white and aqua for a bathroom with spa appeal.

Baths

#123
Match Accessories to the Look

Avoid the temptation to fill a bathroom with lots of tiny knickknacks. Instead, choose a few larger **accessories that contribute color and mood** to your room. The bathroom opposite features a set of five large bamboo vases in layered heights. Three of them are filled with contemporary arrangements of branches to maintain a look that's clean and clutter-free.

#124
Frost for Privacy

Bathroom window treatments can be problematic. You want light but at the same time need to eliminate your neighbor's view of the bathtub. Consider replacing clear glass in exposed windows with **frosted panes**. You could also try a **glass etching cream** or **frosted window film** to let in light but maintain privacy. In some cases, **shutters, café curtains, and top-down shades** can successfully mask lower sections of a window, leaving the top open for light and view.

Fluffy white towels, clean lines, and the Zen-like quality of tall bamboo arrangements create an oasis for relaxation.

#125
Zip up an Old Vanity

Paint an old vanity a fresh new color. Stripe or decoupage the doors—or remove them altogether and place baskets, bins, or stacks of towels on the newly exposed shelves. Shutters or even swing-arm curtain rods (see the example on page 102) can hide the clutter behind short curtains if you wish. While you're at it, **renew drawer pulls** with vintage knobs, a sleek contemporary style, or colorful whimsical designs.

#126
Do Something Different with Towels

Try some of these ideas to **arrange and display towels** in a new way:

- Stack fluffy towels on a chair or bench.

- Roll washcloths and set them on a pretty silver tray.

- Pile folded towels in a big basket set on the floor next to a pedestal sink.

- Throw towels over the rungs of a vintage ladder.

- Hang towels on glass doorknobs or metal coat hooks mounted on a board attached to the wall.

- Attach empty picture frames to the wall using hinges on the top edge and thread towels through the center of the frame.

- Install a behind-the-door towel rack that's perfect for small rooms.

Chapter 12

Kitchens

Kitchen must-haves are changing. Some years ago, custom cabinets were among the few decorator options for a kitchen. Today, granite counters and natural stone floors are all the rage. We're also seeing oversized islands, pot filler spigots by stoves, refrigerator drawers, commercial ranges, custom-fitted drawer inserts, and a wide variety of specialty cabinets, including plate racks, recycling centers, media cabinets, and much more.

One of the most popular requests for a kitchen is an **island**. This can be custom- or ready-made, a simple rolling cart, or an antique farm table, but once it's in place it becomes the center of activity. Before committing to purchase an island, **test sizes** by stacking boxes to the measurements you're considering. Walk around the stack for a week, adjusting the pile to be longer or narrower as required, and you'll develop a good idea of what works.

The **butler's pantry** is back in a big way. If you're fortunate enough to have one in your home, refresh it with paint, lighting, and glass-front cabinet doors. Turn it into an entertaining space by setting up an area for a bar, appetizer service, or buffet. Or give the space a brand new purpose by adding a computer workstation and a desk.

Cabinet woods and finishes are also changing. Oak, preferred by homeowners for many years, is less prevalent; instead, birch, maple, alder, and cherry are popular. Lots of distressed and painted finishes are also in style, which is good news for anyone needing a cabinet makeover. Repainting may take time but, if carefully done, your cabinets can look completely updated.

Decorating a kitchen can be as simple as adding window treatments and a few accessories. After all, many kitchen surfaces and materials can be expensive or difficult to change, so working around these elements is easier and more cost-effective. Yet, as some of the usual decorating standards—fabric, furniture, and accessories—aren't typically as prominent as they are in the rest of the home, kitchens can feel a bit cold.

The preponderance of hard surfaces—flooring, tile, porcelain, stainless steel, porcelain, and glass—may not engender the warm atmosphere you'd like in a kitchen, but you can bring warmth to the space in any number of ways:

- Add touches of wood in flooring or cabinetry
- Use warm colors (yellow, gold, orange, red)
- Bring in fabric window treatments and cushions
- Choose textural accessories
- Put down an an area rug or runner
- Use some freestanding furnishings, like islands, hutches, tables
- Design built-ins, like bookshelves and eating nooks
- Display artwork and collectibles
- Set out fresh flowers and greenery

Enhancing color, pattern, and personality may give your kitchen a new look without the trouble of remodeling. Because kitchens include relatively little wall space, even a bright color may be used without fear of overdoing it. Establish **paint** colors based on fabric and wallpaper, or choose a shade that matches or contrasts with cabinets and accessories.

The kitchen is the hub of most households, so it makes sense to **include a desk area** whenever space permits. Outfit it with a phone, lighting, cookbook shelves, and a few drawers for supplies, and you may just create the most useful spot in the house.

Even small kitchens might accommodate an island as narrow as this one, which offers an extra surface that's perfect for sorting groceries or decorating cookies.

Kitchens

#127
Cabinetscape

Look up! Do your kitchen cabinets have empty space on top? If so, you've just found **a perfect area for display**. Line up similar items, such as a collection of stoneware pitchers or teapots, in neat rows. Group diverse objects in layered clusters with sections of open space between each arrangement. Prop or hang trays, platters, and even artwork against the wall as a backdrop for other collectibles.

#128
Embellish a Backsplash

The area of wall from the cabinets down to the countertop is a prime spot for kitchen decoration. It's the space you probably see most often as you're working, so decorating the backsplash can really make a statement. Consider installing a **tile mural**, patterns of decorative art tiles, or a swath of brightly colored tiles. Do something different by applying embossed tin panels, beadboard, stainless steel tiles, or even a section of mirror.

Fabric and color make the difference in this kitchen makeover. Curtain panels replace cabinet doors, bright window treatments catch our eye, and a deep display shelf shows off colorful collectibles.

#129
Make Room for Comfort

A sitting area in the kitchen makes a great gathering spot. Whether you have an entire family room adjacent to the kitchen or just a corner for a chair and table, it's an area that's likely to become a household favorite. Picture relaxing in a chair with a cup of tea while your spouse chops vegetables. Invite the kids to hang out and read a book while the soup is simmering. This idea could bring your family closer.

#130
Restyle Cabinet Doors

Tired of boring kitchen cabinets? Many cabinet styles **can be revived** with a beauty makeover project:

- Decoupage botanical prints onto cabinet fronts.

- Stencil or paint design motifs onto cabinet doors.

- Cut out a rectangular interior section of the door and install a top and bottom curtain rod inside—shirred with fabric.

- Decorate doors with strips of bamboo, twigs, or molding.

- Replace inset front panels with plain, frosted, ribbed, or leaded glass.

- Replace inset front panels with chicken wire or screening stapled to the back of the door.

Kitchens

#131
Containerize, Organize

Segregate and conquer is the name of the game here. Keep spoons, whisks, and spatulas close to a work area by standing them in an old crock or a shiny stainless steel beaker set next to the stove. Place a pretty tray on the countertop to round up bottles of oil, vinegar, and spices. Bring in a vintage lidded bread tin to hide a clutter of pasta packages and rice for more convenience, more space, more organization.

#132
Find Room for Greenery

Plants bring natural beauty and freshness to a room. Add them in corners, on islands or on top of cabinets to soften a long run of boxy cabinets. Coordinate the plant containers to your room's style—perhaps using vintage tins or ceramic cachepots. Secure artificial greenery in a Styrofoam block disguised under a bit of dried moss. Be sure to clean artificial plants periodically by giving them a quick shower.

#133
Light up Your Work Space

Many kitchens, especially in older homes, need more light. **Shop for under-cabinet fixtures** that directly illuminate work surfaces. **Track lighting** (see page 42) is another good retrofit solution, as are **pendant lights** hung alone or in a line over a countertop or kitchen island. **Strip lighting** and **uplights** increase illumination on top of cabinets.

#134
Go for Granite on a Budget

Granite is a popular countertop choice, but its good looks come with a hefty price tag. Get granite for less by using it in a **select area**—perhaps on a kitchen island or peninsula. Granite **tiles** are also more affordable than a seamless piece of stone. If you don't relish the annual maintenance of granite, then choose an engineered quartz product that mimics granite but offers easy-care style.

Looking for Countertops on the Net
- www.zodiaq.com
- www.silestone.com
- interiordec.about.com
  Search for "Countertops"

A floor of honey-colored wood, a patterned rug, and plants soften the look of all-white cabinets. Books and a collection of blue glass accessories punch up the color quotient.

Kitchens

#135
Hang the Pots

Take attractive kitchenware out of the cupboard and **hang it on a handy pot rack**. A rail system over a stove is one option; a rack suspended from the ceiling is another. Handy homeowners can make their own pot rack using any type of sturdy slatted or grid panel installed to hang from the ceiling. Try a section of old fencing, lengths of a vintage ladder, or a stainless steel grate, then hang pots from heavy S-hooks.

#136
Curb Counter Clutter

Take a good look at your kitchen counters. Kitchen clutter can sometimes multiply to efficiency-clogging proportions. **Give your counters an annual makeover** by clearing everything away. Clean and evaluate each item and leave out only what you use daily. Move seldom-used appliances to out-of-the-way storage. You may gain enough room to set out a bowl of fresh fruit or a vase of flowers.

#137
Update the Floor

New flooring products can update the look of your kitchen in a weekend. Choose a **laminate** that looks like expensive **stone**, yet is much easier to install and maintain. Prefer the look of **wood**? You could put in real hardwood—or go for a lookalike in laminate. Even **tile**, complete with realistic-looking grout lines, has been reproduced in easy-care vinyl and laminate. Want a flooring preview? Use the Design Showcase "Design a Room" feature on the www.armstrong.com Web site.

Sunny yellow cabinets and old ceiling beams steep this kitchen in vintage style. A cheery fireplace, an ambiance-enhancing chandelier, and an inviting farm table also warm and brighten this homey kitchen.

Looking for Lighting on the Internet
- www.shades-of-light.com
- www.lampsplus.com
- www.bellacor.com
- www.americanlightingassoc.com

Chapter 13

Kids' Rooms

Decorating a room for a baby is a happy affair. Months of anticipation and excitement culminate in the day when you finally bring your new little one home.

Beyond the need for a safe environment (you'll definitely want to read up on childproofing), there's the wonderful fun of selecting precious baby wallpaper, tiny ribboned lampshades, and a comfortable rocker or glider chair.

Colors for an infant's room should be those that bring **you** joy. Baby won't know the difference, at least for a while, so feel free to select something you'll take pleasure in seeing many times a day and more than a few times each night! Pastels, whites, neutrals, or brights—any of these might be on target for your sense of nursery style.

Yet baby years are brief. You'll find that the darling teddy bear wallpaper it took weeks to choose may lose its luster as your toddler grows and starts asking for dolls or toy construction vehicles.

How to avoid redoing the **entire** room for each stage of progress? **Go for items that will endure for more than one phase.** Using this approach will save you work and be kinder on your budget.

Such **long-term decorating** involves making lasting choices for the major elements in the room. These include versatile **furnishings** that grow with a child, **paint and wall treatments** that provide a good backdrop for a number of looks to endure from babyhood to preteen years, and functional elements such as **window coverings**, **bookshelves**, **closets**, **and lighting** that will also enhance the room's use over time.

Look for **dual-purpose furnishings**, which are a good **long-term** choice. Some cribs convert to junior-size beds or daybeds that can be used long after baby toys are left behind. Many changing tables morph into dressers that are functional for any age. Even bookcases and armoires are flexible room partners that can as easily hold video games and jeans as diapers and puzzles.

With these important elements in place, turn your attention to the **shorter-term** purchases that are **age appropriate** and that can easily be updated as your child grows. For example, paint the walls in your baby's room a (long-term) sunny yellow color. Put up a (short-term) strippable teddy bear border with matching crib linens. Add fluffy area rugs, baby-themed lamps, and accessories that emphasize the teddy bear motif (all short-term choices).

In a few years, you can effortlessly remove the border and install a new version with images of animals, sports, or whatever captures your child's fancy. Bedding, valances, lamps, and area rugs are also easily switched out for more grown-up looks.

This strategy fills a child's room with a handful of **basic elements** that outlast the short-term touches you'll be able to change as new stages are reached. By accommodating each new period in a growing youngster's life, you'll have a room that pays off in **years of enjoyment**.

Painted cutouts take the place of standard door molding and frame a tantalizing glimpse of the colorful playroom beyond.

The wall color in this child's room is keyed to the upholstery fabric and artwork, yielding a harmonious palette.

Kids' Rooms

#138
Organization Begins in the Closet

Get maximum storage from a child's closet with a closet system. Whether professionally installed or a part of a do-it-yourself kit from a home center, the shelves and fittings are easily adjustable to store clothes as well as toys. Space-saving options, like double- or triple-high hanging rods, drawer units, and corner cabinets, take advantage of every inch. Reconfigure these elements as storage needs change from crib blankets to video games.

#139
Create Kid-Friendly Hideaways

Kids love their own private or **secret spaces.** Build these into a room by segregating part of a large walk-in closet, using the space under an elevated bunk bed, or curtaining off a window seat area for a private reading spot. Playhouses or commercially made play tents are another possibility for a special space that can **encourage imagination**, play, and quiet time.

#140
Decorate the Fifth Wall

Add color and whimsy to a child's room by decorating the ceiling. Lounge on the bed and look up. What would your child like to see every night before going to sleep? You might paint the ceiling a pretty accent color, stencil a border, glue cutouts of stars, or even paint clouds floating across a blue sky. You might like the result so much you'll decide to decorate your own bedroom ceiling! (See an example in the photo on page 109.)

#141
Display It High

Wall-mounted display shelving is a simple project with a big impact. Circle the room with a shelf, mounted about 12 inches (31 cm) below the ceiling and held underneath with shaped wooden shelf brackets. Finish the shelf edge with half-round molding, then paint or stain. Secure everything with L-brackets. **Narrow** shelves show off art, while **deeper** shelving can display books, toys, trophies, and other treasures.

Boost storage potential by outfitting a closet with multi-functional shelves, rods, and bins that can be rearranged to fit baby blankets or teenage collections.

Periwinkle, green, and white are a pretty choice for a baby room, but this space goes further with touches of turquoise and orange to create an unforgettable nursery.

Looking for Kids' Furniture on the Internet

- www.poshtots.com
- www.potterybarnkids.com
- interiordec.about.com
  Search for "Kids"

Make room to dream with furniture arrangements along smaller walls.

Kids' Rooms

#142
Start with the Bed

As in most bedrooms, you can easily use a child's **bedding pattern as a cue** for a color scheme. Try the can't-miss technique of choosing one of the background colors in the bedding pattern to use on walls and floors. Pick out another prominent color to repeat on window treatments, rugs, and furnishings. Finally, repeat the brightest color in the small accents, such as artwork and accessories.

#143
Improvise Versatility

Reversible comforters can provide a second look for an older child's bedroom. Turn to the dinosaur side for your toddler, then reverse to the striped side while grandma is staying in the room. A plain white down comforter is perfect for older kids. Simply insert it into a series of colorful duvet covers—featuring fire trucks, soccer balls, then race cars—as they grow.

#144
Paint It Out

When a child's room is very small, consider **painting the furniture** the same color as the walls. This helps the furniture to visually recede a bit, making the room feel just a little larger. Pale colors, such as buttercream, rosy pink, white, or icy blue, can also add to the illusion of more space. Apply this color technique to window treatments, flooring, and rugs as well.

#145
Light Block the Windows

Window treatments that provide maximum light-blocking and privacy may help small children sleep longer or get to bed earlier when it is still light outside. Room-darkening roller shades are the simplest and cheapest solution, but some miniblinds and fabric shades also offer **light-blocking options**. Curtains and shades can be constructed with a room-darkening liner, effectively blocking all light when drawn.

Kids' Rooms

#146
A Wall of Shelves Can Hold It All

When a child's bedroom can spare 10 inches (25 cm) or more along one wall, installing **built-in bookshelves and cabinets** is a great idea. Perfect even for smaller rooms, built-ins pack a lot of storage into a small footprint. Don't want to construct built-ins? Line up ready-made bookshelf units instead, attaching them securely to the wall and to each other. If you wish, finish the edges with lengths of molding for a more built-in look.

#147
Lounge around in a Child's Room

Kids love to lounge when reading, playing, or daydreaming. Include cushioned window seats, pint-size beanbag chairs, or squishy floor pillows to supply lounging comfort with kid-friendly style. Make these with washable, preshrunk zip-off covers to facilitate easy cleaning. Be sure to update these furnishings as your child grows—trading in toddler-scaled items for full-size upholstered seating as well as ergonomically designed desk chairs for teens.

#148
Frame Works by the House Artist

Purchase a set of large **Plexiglas box picture frames** in standard sizes. Fit pieces of colored acid-free matboard into each frame and insert your child's latest artistic endeavors. Use artist's tape or rubber cement to keep the pictures straight on the mat. Change the artwork now and then for a colorful evolving display in your child's room, hall, guest room, or other prominent location.

#149
Play Rugs Add Fun

Add an invigorating shot of color and pattern to a young child's room with a **whimsical play rug**. Available in designs that include street scenes, world maps, alphabets, and the solar system, such rugs can inspire both play and learning. Many styles are large and may be most appropriate in play areas with an open floor area so the rug's illustrations aren't obscured by furniture. See www.kidsrugs.com for more ideas.

Offering storage, seating, and display in one neat package, built-ins make a handsome and useful addition to a child's room.

Chapter 14

Home Offices

When I was a child, my dad had a small desk in the corner of his bedroom. A few years later, he built a closet along one wall of the living room and filled it with shelving and a long work surface that could be hidden behind large doors. Much later, after moving into a new home, he had a separate home office, eventually rearranging it to hold two desks, computers, printers, and a big closet full of supplies and filing cabinets.

This progression of solutions over the years may parallel your own needs for a home office. Maybe your tiny dorm desk was abandoned for a board-and-block table in a first apartment, then for a full-size desk in your first home. Perhaps now you telecommute or run a home business and need workspace and functional furnishings in a room apart from everyday family activities.

While a separate room devoted to a home office is the ideal situation for some, this generous allocation of space is not always possible, as smaller homes and apartments may not have an extra room to spare. **Dual-purpose rooms** are one solution where, for example, you might use a guestroom for an office whenever it isn't hosting guests.

Yet even without obvious options for dual-purpose rooms, there may be **nooks of space** where a desk can be constructed or purchased to fit. Look for these kinds of spaces in any **under-utilized areas** of your home.

For instance:

- On a wide stair landing
- In a finished attic or basement
- At the end of a hallway
- In a bedroom
- A corner of the dining room
- Inside a converted closet
- An office armoire in a bedroom
- A side table in a living room

One of these spaces may fill the need for a suitable work area for bills and the paperwork involved in running a home.

Despite optimistic predictions of a **paperless society**, we now get as much mail in a week as our great grandparents received in a year. We have more bills, more receipts, more address lists, more school papers, and more tax files than ever before.

A large home office will have room for plenty of file cabinets. Choose sturdy file drawers made for commercial use, and avoid inexpensive filing units that can be flimsy and frustrating to use.

In a smaller home you may need to store supplies and archived files in a location away from the desk area. Plastic or cardboard file boxes are a good solution for this type of storage. Set them on shelves in a closet or attic, making sure they are well labeled.

Where will you put your home office?
Depending on your particular space needs, there's probably at least one workable location for a useful office area. Take a look, it might be right in front of you.

Pulling the desk away from the wall allows easy passage on both sides.
Modular pieces like these can be rearranged to meet changing needs.

Home Offices

#150
Choose a Table

Any table of desk height—about 30 inches (76 cm)—can serve as a work surface. Alternatives include kitchen and dining tables, library tables, and sofa tables, which can be used anywhere in the home. Accessorize them simply to match the décor of the room, adding covered containers to hold often-used tools or supplies. Keep overflow office equipment in a nearby chest or closet.

#151
Choose a Chair Based on Use

How long do you plan to sit at your desk? If you'll only perch long enough to dash off a note or write a check, then almost any chair will do. Longer sessions for extensive phoning or online research **require a chair that is ergonomically correct**. Test chairs in an office furniture store, and purchase a fully adjustable model to make working as comfortable as possible.

#152
Center a Desk

Tired of looking at the wall while you work? **Place your desk** so it's **perpendicular to a wall** or even in the **center** of the room (like the one on page 117). Position it with a view of the door or windows. Cord control can be more difficult, so run wires under the desktop or into a cord-management system. Add a credenza or storage armoire to the room, and you're in business.

#153
Hide It with Fabric

Slipcovering an unattractive desk is a great way to disguise a desk's less-than-perfect finish or style by sewing together two flat panels of fabric. One piece should be the size of the desktop (plus seam allowances). The other length of fabric will function as the skirt and is attached around three sides of the top panel. Leave one side open (without a skirt) for knee room and access to drawers. Top with glass for a smooth work surface. Choose fabric that coordinates with your room, or look for fun faux leathers or suede.

Integrate a work area into any room by choosing attractive furnishings and stashing the clutter inside cabinets or a nearby closet.

Home Offices

#154
Shut the Door on Work

Armoire desks are one of the great inventions for a space-saving home office. They'll store everything in one place, hide the cords and clutter, and offer furniture good looks when you close the doors at the end of the day. Browse for styles that accommodate the way you work, including your computer configuration and storage requirements.

#155
Keep Clutter Under Wraps

Unless you enjoy a cluttered look or are able to keep your work area super-neat, you'll want to **opt for closed storage near the desk**. This means shelves and cabinets with doors so items are concealed. Large lidded baskets or boxes are another possibility. Under long runs of open counter, it's sometimes possible to install shelving under the countertop at knee level and hang fabric panels to hide it.

#156
Commandeer a Closet

Convert a clothes closet into a desk area by removing the doors and clothes rod and installing a desktop, shelves, and lighting. Adjustable shelves give you the option of sizing each shelf perfectly for paper, files, or computer boxes. They'll also give you a way to convert the closet back to clothes storage by taking out the shelves and refitting a clothes pole into the design.

#157
Do-It-Yourself Desks

Build your own desk from any flat panel, such as a hollow-core door, a length of wood, or a laminate countertop. Rest this on a pair of sturdy bookcases or two-drawer file cabinets for an instant desk that is custom sized to your specifications. Some surfaces may require a layer of glass on top to create a perfectly smooth surface.

Conceal an office inside an armoire designed to hold computer equipment and supplies.

Make the most of a home office by
installing multiple workstations.

Home Offices

#158
Consider Workstation Needs

Do the kids commandeer your desk for homework right when you wanted to use it? If so, it might be time to **consider a multiworkstation home office space**. Put in more than one desk, or install lengths of countertop to give everyone room to spread out. Consider putting in a home network so each user can share the Internet connection and printers.

#159
Add Personality

From collections to art to family photos, **personal touches give your office a bit of character**. No room for a big display? Set an open book of photographs in a book holder to show off pictures that inspire you. A bulletin board or magnetic board might hold postcards and mementos. In a larger office space, hang a few oversize pieces of art for maximum impact with minimal fuss.

#160
Sorting with the Reach Test

Submit each office item to the reach test before putting it away. If you need an object daily, place it where you can easily reach it without getting out of your chair. When an item is needed infrequently, place it in appropriate storage areas, closer or farther away from your work area, as needed.

Looking for Office Furniture on the Internet
- www.calclosets.com
- www.ikea.com
- interiordec.about.com
  Search for "Home Offices"

Chapter 15
Halls

This classic chest is timeless, traditional, and functional. Here, a painting and a few accessories keep it company. A mirror hung over the chest would yield a different effect.

Like the bullet train, the Autobahn, and Route 66, a hallway is designed to take us from one location to another. It's a **transition space** where we generally linger just long enough to straighten a picture or drop the mail.

Too often, halls are dark and uninviting. Without windows to decorate or much room for furniture, we need to find other ways to give hallways personality. Our challenge is to infuse them with light, color, and **eye appeal**.

The hall—including foyer, stairwells, and passages throughout the home—can either be **a preview** or an area that **unites every space** it connects. Because halls open up to adjoining rooms, they often complement the colors and styles in those adjacent spaces. And, as we don't spend much time in a hall, we can sometimes afford to be bolder with color and artwork. Even people who are shy about color may enjoy short bursts of intense color in pass-through spaces.

Besides color, the single most important element of hallway décor is **lighting**. Consider yourself fortunate when a hall has lots of windows (like the rooms shown on the next few pages). But if there are none, bring more light to the space with some of these tried-and-true decorating techniques:

- Add more light with additional electrical fixtures (see tip #164).

- Install electrified wall sconces.

- Put up a big mirror or a collection of mirrors for glitter (see tip #166).

- Use landscape art that includes a distant horizon (see tip #170).

- Paint the walls with low-sheen satin paint rather than flat.

- Apply silver leaf or metallic paint to the ceiling.

- Install a skylight.

Pieces of **occasional furniture** make an entry or wide hallway more attractive and improve function as well. A chest like the one on the opposite page is a pleasing classic, yet other options are numerous. A pair of chairs and a pedestal table look wonderful, but a bench, sofa table, or sideboard also gives useful service. Narrow passageways are not often able to accommodate full-size furnishing; a simple row of peg hooks for coats and a narrow bench may suffice.

Smaller halls can be decorated delightfully even though space is at a premium. Once color and light are added, consider hanging slender art shelves to hold a changing array of prints. **Artwork** becomes especially important in windowless areas. A savvy selection of paintings and prints can bring in **the look of the outdoors**, giving the impression you've opened a window into the room (see the example on page 91).

Bring **color**, **light**, **and art** into your hallways, and you'll enjoy passing through these spaces every day.

Halls

#161
Furnish for Interest

Wider halls and foyers can get a big **boost of personality** by adding furniture. A round pedestal table is a classic foyer option that lends grace and style. Chests, sideboards, and narrow tables also make useful companions in an entry or hallway. You might also add a place to sit (on chairs or benches), built-ins for storage or display, coat trees, hat racks, or even an armoire if there's room.

#162
Showcase Collectibles

A hallway can be a great place to **display a collection**. Fitting wider halls with custom display shelving is a good answer for power collectors who are still accumulating objects. Floor-to-ceiling shelves can be of any depth required, from mere inches for model trains or miniatures to deeper styles for books or glassware. Review lighting needs so displays are lit to best advantage.

#163
Paint the Unexpected

The ceiling in a hall is the perfect place to **add the unexpected**. One simple solution is to paint it with a touch of color, such as butter yellow, sky blue, or blush pink. Another is to **stencil** a geometric border. If the ceiling's surface is smooth and in good condition, a semigloss or **metallic paint** will reflect light and add a bit of shine. Alternatively, give your ceiling a fanciful touch with faux sky or a mural of leaves and vines.

The sight of a beautiful pedestal table welcomes guests. A center hall table like this one is the perfect spot to display a seasonal plant or a vase of fresh flowers.

Looking for Paint on the Internet
- www.glidden.com
- www.paintideas.com
- interiordec.about.com

  Search for "Paint"

Halls

#164
Punch Up Drama with Lighting

Interesting **pools of light** add drama to an interior hallway. Install recessed lighting or lengths of track lighting, aiming the fixtures down or toward the wall. Wall-mounted sconces offer similar illumination from a different perspective. In one-story homes, a skylight or Solatube (see www.solatube.com) will flood even the darkest hall with natural light during the day.

#165
Design a Gallery

Think of a hall as a gallery, and you give a new purpose to the space. Hang a row of framed art photographs, botanical prints, or movie posters, and light them from above. Columns and pedestals are another great gallery space option to lift sculptures and large accessories to a place of importance.

#166
Open Up!

Narrow spaces will get a boost from **reflective surfaces** such as mirrors or gloss and metallic paints. Open, **airy color palettes** including neutrals and pastels and some open wallpaper patterns can also give the room more perceived space. **See-through** tabletops of Lucite or glass make furniture practically disappear. Finally, **reducing intrusions** (like large pieces of furniture) in a space keeps the eye moving forward as well.

#167
Install a Wall of Art

Wall-mounted art shelves can work in the narrowest of hallways, providing a place to **display posters, prints, or collectibles**. They feature a slim ledge where framed or unframed photos and prints can lean casually against the wall. One long shelf can draw visitors forward into a room, while a number of shorter shelves can be hung in a focal point area. Again, illuminate the art for the greatest impact.

A line of ceiling lights invites us into this space while a vase of curly willow on a pedestal accents the view with texture.

Halls

#168
Saturated Colors Add Richness

Midtoned, bright, and darker paints can be used successfully in a hallway when the ceiling, door trim, and molding are kept very light or white. In the absence of natural light, add enough artificial light—using a mix of wall sconces and recessed or track lights—to light the space well; you don't want it to feel like a cave. Bring more interest to the area with art.

#169
Push Up the Ceiling with Vertical Lines

Emphasize vertical lines in spaces that have lower ceilings to **increase the sense of height**. Tall accessories (such as the twigs in vases on page 56) are one way to do this. Vertically **striped** wall treatments are another. Look for artwork that is **taller** than it is wide or that includes vertical lines, such as tall trees, in the subject matter. Hanging pictures in **vertical arrangements**, one over another, is another useful technique.

#170
Use Art in Place of a Window

Murals and landscape art can serve as "windows" in a hallway or other windowless spaces. Use photographs, prints, murals, and other types of landscapes that draw the viewer into the picture and offer a look at a **wide vista or faraway horizon**. See examples on pages 53 and 91.

#171
Create a Far-End Focal Point

Introduce a focal point to a hallway by placing an object of interest at the far end. A chest or sculpture can fill the bill nicely. Make sure it is well lit. If the end of your hall has no space for furniture, hang a piece of **artwork** illuminated by a picture light, or paint a **mural** directly onto the wall.

Fanciful touches—yellow walls, a twig railing, detailed sconce, and artwork—give personality to what could have been a lackluster transition space to the second floor.

Looking for Art on the Internet
- www.artselect.com
- www.art.com
- www.allposters.com

Chapter 16

Accessories

If you've never been able to fully nail down your **decorating style**, it may help to consider your taste in **accessories**.

Look around at objects you've already accumulated, or think about accessories you'd like to have. These items can be **powerful clues** to what you find appealing, and they'll often direct the way to a particular style. Are your accessories vintage glass or stainless steel? Ceramic plates or giant baskets? Asian chests or Indian pottery? Vintage architectural elements or elegant oil paintings?

Contemplate a **natural progression** from your favorite accessories to the furnishings you'll be choosing for your home. Have you consistently selected formal objects, modern art, or rustic collectibles? Is a theme of color, motif, or style repeated? Do you always choose antiques over new objects, or vice versa? Perhaps this accumulation of treasured objects is leading you toward a classic formal look, a comfortable casual style, or a French-inspired country design. The style they indicate is worthy of further consideration.

Accessories are prized for their versatility and can be rearranged on a whim for daily living as well as special occasions. A **prop closet** is the perfect place to hold the objects not currently on display. Items such as vases, candles, cachepots, bowls, and trays can safely hide here until they're needed.

When the crisp days of autumn roll around, you can replace summery floral accessories with fall accent pieces that are darker and richer. Months later, when spring beckons, you can pull out your lighter and brighter accessories again.

A prop closet should contain practical items as well—flower-arranging supplies, tacky wax, felt dots, scissors, picture hooks, wire, and so on. A supply of these **mechanics**, along with a **toolbox** of essentials (tape measure, wire clippers, level, and hammer), can make it quick and easy to create new arrangements of accessories throughout your home.

Remember, too, that **accessories add color** to a room, so don't choose everything in taupe and brown unless they're the basis of your color scheme. Generally, accessories should repeat other colors in the room, often highlighting the brightest colors in your palette.

Plants may be the most inexpensive and versatile accessories of all. They soften and bring a feeling of life to a room. Use them in corners, atop tall armoires, on bookshelves, or on coffee tables. Live plants are beautiful, but if you don't have the time or desire to care for plants, try the many excellent artificial alternatives. Arranged in beautiful containers, they make good stand-ins for live plants.

As you continue to collect accessories over the years, be sure each new purchase **supports the overall style** of your home. Hold to the theme of a country interior with accessories of wood, baskets, stone, vintage architectural elements, twig pieces, pottery, antique boxes, and so on. Underscore a more formal home with items of silver, crystal, porcelain, china, fine woods, gilt mirrors, and the like.

This **consistency** of style or theme makes it easy to mix and match objects throughout your home, creating harmonious displays whenever you're in the mood to rearrange.

Dashes of cinnamon and deep red relate the accessories
to the fabrics and upholstery in this cozy living room.

Accessories

#172
Lift It Up

Look for objects that can **elevate accessories** to pleasing heights. While acrylic display stands are available, their starkly commercial aura doesn't fit every décor. Try stacks of **books, pedestals, and boxes**. All of these lift accessories off the table so arrangements are more interesting to view.

#173
Easy Centerpieces with Versatility

Collect a few **large accessory pieces** to use as centerpieces for your dining room table. These should be large enough to stand alone but should not overpower the table. A **soup tureen** looks lovely alone, but it can also be filled with a green plant. A large **footed bowl** or beautiful platter can host a fragrant display of lemons, beaded fruit, or seeded spheres.

#174
Get Creative with Twigs

Bare branches set into tall vases make a big statement (see page 56 for an example). Set these on either side of a mantle or in a foyer. Large arrangements also fill empty corners. Obtain curly willow twigs, bamboo stalks, and rustic branches from a florist or a craft store. You can also select tree trimmings from your own backyard for an accessory that's practically free.

#175
Encircling Style

Wreaths are classic and pleasing. **Make a wreath** to adorn your home by attaching silk or dried leaves with hot glue on a grapevine wreath of any size. Embellish with silk flowers, berries, and an elegant ribbon. Hang it over a mantle, in a hallway, or on a door. A trio of wreaths can stand in for artwork, while small wreaths look wonderful in casual rooms hanging at the back of bookshelves behind other collectibles.

Stacks of items fill this generous coffee table with interesting vignettes. Vases of greenery are an easy way to showcase garden cuttings, which often last longer than fresh flowers.

Accessories

#176
Make an Impact

Think big! **Large accessories** have presence and can give a room elegance, scale, and interest. Avoid the common mistake of setting out too many tiny accessories, as small objects are rarely noticed from across a room. You might, for example, forego purchasing a set of small ceramic vases in favor of one terrific piece that can really make a statement.

#177
Odd Numbers Create Interest

Add the rule of threes to your decorating repertoire. While symmetrical displays create balance, arranging **odd numbers** of objects adds interest—three boxes on a shelf, five plates on a wall, seven tall candlesticks on the mantle. Try it in your own home. Set two objects on your coffee table. Now add a third item. You'll find that a grouping of three, five, or seven is generally more pleasing than an arrangement of two, four, or six.

#178
Boost Storage Capacity with Containers

Anyone who lives in a smaller home should **make storage a consideration** whenever shopping for decorative accessories. Items such as boxes and baskets are perfect candidates, as they look good *and* provide hiding places for everyday items. Use them to house CDs, games, notecards, coasters, maps, or whatever needs to be hidden from view. You might also adjust existing shelves to accommodate a row of identical baskets that can house toys, books, or magazines.

#179
Simplicity Makes a Statement

Give outstanding accessories **breathing room**. This allows their beautiful form, unique color, or interesting texture to be fully seen and appreciated. Consider how a museum displays every object as a singular treasure, leaving ample open space to emphasize its beauty and significance. A lovely fern on a tall plant stand, a large sculpture atop a column, and a vase of flowers on your dining room table are all examples of this technique.

An uncluttered display of accessories exhibits the harmonious result of sticking to a color scheme. The contrast of light and dark, along with simple, deliberate placement, commands the viewer's attention.

The numerous accessories in this living room are displayed in a mix of symmetrical and asymmetrical arrangements. Hints of gold and brass unite many of the objects on the far wall.

Accessories

#180
Build Height

Build height into an arrangement of accessories with tall vases, lamps, and floral displays. Flat objects, such as plates, photos, and trays, can be propped upright in plate stands or placed on a wall. Framed artwork can be hung behind or set into display stands and incorporated into a table or bookshelf arrangement.

#181
Frame It in Similar Finishes

Collecting picture **frames in one color or finish**, such as wood, brass, silver, or pewter, allows easy groupings and regroupings on walls, tables, and piano tops. The frames can vary in detail and size, or they might be identical. Look for a style that complements your home's furnishings. Mats inside frames should be acid-free to avoid damage to photographs or pictures. Consult a local framer for advice and options.

#182
Display in Levels

Traditional table arrangements place items in **high**, **medium**, **and low** positions. A tall object, such as a lamp, anchors the grouping. Next, fill in the space between the bottom of the lampshade and the tabletop with a plant or a plate set upright on a plate stand. Finally, set a low object in front—a small box, figurine, or bowl, for example. Infinite variations of this technique can guide the creation of pleasing arrangements.

This well-bred table of accessories expresses a look that's classic and sumptuous. Notice the pleasing regression of height from the top of the lamp down to the smallest box.

Chapter 17

Vintage Décor

What is vintage? Any item from the past that does not qualify as antique (a true antique is always more than one hundred years old) can be termed vintage. A side table from the 1940s, a framed mirror from the 1930s, or colorful kitchen textiles from the 1950s all qualify as vintage. China, glassware, art, furniture, kitchenware, chandeliers, and holiday decorations are also prized finds.

Decorating with vintage pieces may be as popular for the **feelings** they evoke as the actual **style** elements. Things that are imperfect, tattered, crackled, worn, and full of character— these fascinating vintage finds tug at our heartstrings, yet often make only a small dent in our pocketbooks. Rachel Ashwell's famous Shabby Chic style has renewed our collective interest in vintage items. As we recycle, reuse, and repurpose items discarded as irrelevant, we **give them new life** and renewed appreciation.

Where can you find vintage? **Flea markets**, **secondhand stores**, **garage sales**, and Aunt Pauline's **attic** are the usual sources. **Online auctions** like eBay offer gold mines of vintage treasures for the bidding. **Antique malls**, **country fairs**, and **tag sales** are more sources for vintage collectibles.

For anyone who is new to flea market shopping, a few tips are in order:

- Learn the ropes by tagging along on a flea market shopping trip with a friend.

- Wear comfortable clothes and shoes.

- **Carry cash**, small bills, checks, and ID.

- Carry a **measured floorplan** of your home, especially if you're looking for art or furnishings to fit a certain location.

- Take your **paint and fabric swatches** to help match colors.

- Take a **tape measure**.

- Set a **budget** limit before you go, but consider how much to go over it if you happen upon just the right item.

- If you plan to buy furniture, bring your largest vehicle, along with blankets and rope.

- Browse for **one type** of item (floral china, for example) to avoid feeling overwhelmed by the range of merchandise.

- If you love it, **buy it now**; it may be gone later.

- Not sure how to **negotiate**? Some dealers take 10 percent off for the asking. Learn the lingo by listening to other shoppers come to terms with sellers.

- Carry a large **tote bag** to hold small purchases, or use a wagon or rolling cart to haul heavy items, such as dishes.

- Know how much wear and tear you can tolerate on a piece and say no to a purchase if living with the flaws or fixing it is not within your reach.

Search for pieces that speak to you—the items that practically reach out across the aisle and beg you to take them home. These are the treasures that make your home a unique reflection of your personality.

Lots of vintage finds can be displayed as is, while others need refurbishing or repairs. Books on flea market shopping often include tips on refinishing these bargains of old furniture and accessories.

The vintage-style rooms on the following pages illustrate how to incorporate vintage finds into a space. Your home is full of life and activity, not a museum, so integrating these interesting pieces into your décor may be the best way to honor their unspoken legacy of beauty and function.

Vintage items you can use everyday—like the dinner and glassware shown here—are lots of fun to collect.

If you've ever thought that vintage décor is synonymous with clutter, this bedroom will change your mind. Restraint keeps the style clean, simple, and refreshing.

Vintage Décor

#183
Give White New Interest

Not sure if you want an all-white room? You can use lots of white but **inject more personality by bringing in vintage items**. A small table, a refurbished chandelier, accessories, and colorful pillows bring an all-white space to life and anchor a room that could otherwise appear to float away.

#184
Add Vintage Style with Art

Count on **vintage artwork** or reproductions to add old-time charm to an interior. Old watercolors and oil paintings are favorites, but budget alternatives include vintage postcards, book illustrations, and magazine covers. Add a vintage look to a laundry room by framing old advertisements for soap, or charm a kitchen with colorful produce packing crate labels.

#185
Increase the Architectural IQ

Want to impart **an instantly homey feel** to a room? Salvaged architectural pieces can do it with ease. Cracked and crazed building components, old windows, corbels, gates, fence posts, and other architectural elements impart texture, pattern, and interest. Arrange smaller items on a tabletop with a plant or a stack of books, or hang pieces on the wall as vintage art.

#186
Research Your Vintage

To get a specific look, research the vintage style of your choice on the Internet, in magazines, or in books devoted to your particular vintage passion. Many offer a wealth of knowledge about condition and values and offer tips on care and repair. Note the patterns, colors, and motifs for a particular vintage era, and begin to acquire those items that appeal to you.

Vintage Décor

#187
Don't Store Vintage Pieces—Use Them!

Look for objects that can show off **beautiful vintage style** *and* earn their keep. A collectible bowl, pitcher, urn, or mug can be home to a green plant or a flower arrangement. Vintage plates can be hung on a wall or set on a plate stand as art. Old wooden corbels can serve as bookends or unique shelf supports, and a vintage picture frame may be reinvented as a mirror, tray, or bulletin board.

#188
Finish It Off with Hardware

Antique or reproduction **hardware** is essential in a vintage room. Glass doorknobs, window hardware, vintage drawer pulls, and elaborate coat hooks can add just the right detail. To find hardware for your project, search antique shops in your area or look online for vintage hardware sources, including Liz's Antique Hardware at www.lahardware.com.

#189
Open the Door to New Uses for Doors

Invent new uses for **vintage doors** to show off their time-worn dents and layers of crackled paint. Hinge two or three doors together to make a folding screen. Hang a door horizontally on the wall as a headboard for a daybed. Outfit a door panel with a narrow shelf and a handful of coat hooks to create a useful hat rack in an entry area.

#190
Look through Rose-Colored Windows

Embellish any window in your home with a **vintage stained-glass panel**. These old panels can be suspended from the top of the window frame with eyehooks and strong nylon line or simply set on the sill. Their color and pattern impart unique architectural style to even ordinary windows and look wonderful from outside as well as inside. Find stained glass at antique stores or on eBay's Web site at www.eBay.com.

Monochromatic creams and browns make an appropriately muted backdrop for this collection of vintage objects.

Vintage Décor

#191
Choose Light Fixtures to Fit

Lighting is a great way to convey vintage style. You may find just the thing at an antique fair, on eBay, or on the Internet at Vintage Lighting (www.vintagelighting.com) or any of the other online sources. Many older pieces are rewired and restored, making them a viable alternative for a vintage-style home.

#192
Show Off a Theme

For personality and interest, nothing beats a **themed display**. Bring together vintage items that relate to a specific color, style, or object. Group a collection of items using the high-medium-low technique (see tip #182), placing larger items at the back and smaller things at the front. Alternatively, simply set your treasures close together, like the bridge-themed objects shown opposite or the dog-themed accessories pictured on page 150.

#193
Functioning Kitchen Style

Reconditioned **kitchen appliances** add the look of yesteryear with the function you need in today's kitchens. Antique stoves, for example, offer a variety of useful features, such as warming ovens, accessories, and shelves that aren't found in many of their modern cousins. Flea markets, junk stores, and used appliance dealers may offer reconditioned models buffed up to look good as new. Browse Antique Stove Heaven (www.antiquestoveheaven.com) for inspiration.

Combine one part tin lantern, one part vintage mantle, one part red wall, and one part fascinating bridge memorabilia to yield a most intriguing room.

Looking for Vintage on the Internet
- www.ebay.com
- www.tias.com
- interiordec.about.com
  Search for "Flea Market"

Chapter 18

Collections

It has been said that you can learn a lot about a person by knowing what they collect. If so, **what do your collections say about you**? Are you whimsical, casual, well-traveled, sophisticated? Do you love a certain style, a particular color, or a specific motif? Do you adore the elegant, or are you someone who loves contemporary, country, or rustic? Are your collections formally displayed in symmetrical perfection, or do they live casually in the thick of a busy household?

I imagine that if you collect sterling silver, for instance, I would find your home filled with elegant appointments in a formal setting. If you collect ceramic cookie jars, perhaps I'd find a home that is warm and welcoming, filled with the aroma of freshly baked treats. A modern art collector's home might show off a minimal, bold, and contemporary flair.

No matter your unique choice, what you collect often has an enormous impact on your home. The color, style, and size of a collection play a role in determining how it is displayed. A collection of twenty-five small paperweights can comfortably sit on a coffee table or tray, while the same number of vintage teapots would require a much larger space.

The collector's personality also plays a role. You may choose to casually arrange a colorful collection of glassware on a bookshelf, while someone else would keep it securely locked in a china cabinet. One person may make frequent use of silver vases for fresh flower arrangements; another may keep them tucked away and never used. Are you more inclined to use or display?

While very **large collections** are impressive, some may need to be culled and displayed in a way that underscores the importance of each piece. **Small collections**, on the other hand, should be kept together, building attractive vignettes of focused attention.

Art collectors often have strong opinions about how art should be seen. If you're new to art collection, these general guidelines on **making art important** will get you started:

- Display art in a focal point of the room.

- Light artwork well with a picture light or overhead lighting.

- Always frame art with acid-free archival materials and techniques.

- Use extra-wide matting or framing to give importance to smaller prints.

- Hang art over a contrasting wall color for maximum impact.

- Set a painting on a freestanding easel.

- Arrange collections of art in groupings for greatest effect.

If your collectibles are hidden in a box or cupboard, consider how to shelve or showcase them. Devoting an entire breakfront to a collection, like the one on page 153, gives a collection real emphasis. Breaking a large collection into pretty vignettes scattered throughout the house is another technique.

Bring out those hidden treasures, dust them off, and enjoy viewing them. Let your collections speak volumes about your style.

An eye-catching assortment of shapes increases interest as ample natural light illuminates this collection of pretty glassware.

It's not hard to identify the theme that captures this homeowner's heart. Dog images carry through from the painting to the accessories, forming a cohesive display.

Collections

#194
Bring It Together

Do you have more than four similar objects? If so, then you have the beginnings of a collection. However, a small collection may hardly be noticeable if it's spread all over the house. Whenever possible, **keep collectibles together for the greatest impact**. This applies to artwork as well as accessories and is especially true when a collection consists of only a few objects.

#195
Employ Contrast to Boost Interest

Utilize the **principles of contrast** to display collections. Often, an **accent color used behind** the objects will give them much more impact than they have on their own. A collection of embossed white plates in front of a white wall can be overlooked, yet if the same plates are displayed in front of a pretty rosy pink or cobalt blue background, their form and color may be enhanced.

#196
Vary the Location

When you **collect decorative objects**, such as plates, books, and artwork, they can double as accessories in your home. **Rotate pieces** in a large collection so you can enjoy them all over the house. Display a few pieces on a sideboard, some on the mantle, and more on the dining room table. As you move objects around to new locations, you'll find your appreciation for each piece is renewed.

#197
Serve Them on a Tray

Group small objects on trays to keep them contained and displayed together. The tray can be easily lifted for dusting or removed altogether for parties or the holidays. Collections that fit on trays include paperweights, small porcelain boxes, and framed family photos. Choose a tray with a color and style that doesn't compete with the collection.

Collections

#198
Mix It Up

Don't underestimate the **appeal of diversity** in a display. When everything is nicely arranged but seems a bit flat, try adding **something different**. Objects made of metal, glass, ceramic, or wood may be the perfect counterpoint. Natural elements, such as fruit and greenery, are another versatile means of punching up an arrangement of treasured objects.

#199
Best-Dressed Shelves

Dress up plain shelves with runners, fabric pieces, lace, or placemats to add color. **Shelf edging**—strips of paper ribbon or lace trim used to decorate the front shelf edge—is another way to bump up interest. The backs of shelves can be decorated with wallpaper, contrasting paint, or fabric.

#200
Bring on the Complements

Complementary colors can make collectibles sing. Picture an arrangement of gorgeous orange lilies in a cobalt blue vase or a pile of fresh green apples on a painted red tray. Each color brings out the best in the other, brightening the entire display. Complementary combinations include orange and blue, red and green, and yellow and purple.

#201
Inspire with Dancing Light

Collections of china and glassware may be overlooked when set in a dark bookcase, yet they'll sparkle and shine when lit well from above, underneath, or behind. You can also **set glass pieces on a sunny windowsill** where they'll be appreciated from both inside and outside the house and cast dancing prisms of light on interior walls.

A mix of large and small collectibles is embellished with accents of yellow and white. The relaxed symmetry of the arrangement is punctuated by whimsical pieces, brass, glass, and a small oil painting.

PURE LARD

PURE MILK

Resources

One miracle of the Internet is that it never closes. Whether you're home at midnight or on a break at work, you can browse for information or comparison shop quickly and easily. It's great fun to meander through home decorating Web sites, looking at styles and colors, printing out items of interest, and bookmarking your favorites. Even if you don't own a computer, you can readily log on to one at a library or Internet café.

Internet browsing opens new possibilities in home decorating, enabling access to endless product choices. There's no need to drive all over town, going from store to store, hoping to find the one item you need. You might still shop locally, but previewing products online lets you know about sizes, features, and prices before you set foot outside your door. Merchandise not needing an in-person assessment can be instantly ordered and delivered to your door with a minimum of hassle.

Some online decorating sites offer information, tips, and project instructions. Some are strictly shopping sites, with either a full or partial retail selection for sale online. Others feature photos of their current product lines that must be purchased elsewhere, either in retail stores or through trade sources, such as interior designers and architects.

The sites listed represent a small fraction of home decorating sites available on the Web, and they demonstrate the scope of information that's right at your fingertips. Start exploring home décor here. Given the changing nature of our world, however, don't be surprised if you come across a site that's under reconstruction or no longer valid. Mergers and altered business plans mean that sites evolve, grow, and sometimes close down. Even when this happens, more than a handful of similar sites are still eager for your attention.

You'll find it worthwhile to understand more about searching the Internet using a search portal like About.com or a search engine like Google. Look for a link titled "Advanced Search"—a feature that can better target results to help find the information you need.

Decorating Information

Better Homes and Gardens
www.bhg.com

Country Home Magazine
www.countryhome.com

Decorating on About.com
http://interiordec.about.com

DIY Net Projects
www.diynet.com

Home and Garden Television
www.hgtv.com

Homestore.com
www.homestore.com

Home Portfolio
www.homeportfolio.com

House Beautiful
www.housebeautiful.com

iVillage: Home and Garden/Decorate
www.ivillage.com

Southern Living Magazine
www.southernliving.com

Accessories

Ballard Designs
www.ballarddesigns.com

Crate and Barrel
www.crateandbarrel.com

Exposures
www.exposuresonline.com

Pottery Barn
www.potterybarn.com

Spiegel Catalog
www.spiegel.com

Restoration Hardware
www.restorationhardware.com

Art

All Posters
www.allposters.com

Art.com
www.art.com

Art Select
www.artselect.com

Barewalls.com
www.barewalls.com

Frame Your Art
www.frameyourart.com

NextMonet
www.nextmonet.com

PaintingsDirect
www.paintingsdirect.com

Baths

Dornbracht
www.dornbracht.com

HansGrohe
www.hansgrohe-usa.com

Kohler
www.kohler.com

Links on Baths
http://interiordec.about.com

National Kitchen and Bath
www.nkba.org

Rejuvenation
www.rejuvenation.com

Rohl
www.rohlhome.com

Soho Corp
www.sohocorp1.com

Umbra
www.umbra.com

Waterworks
www.waterworks.com

Bath and Kitchen Tile

Ann Sacks Tile
www.annsackstile.com

Elon
www.elon.co.uk

Euro Tile
www.euro-tile.com

Home Portfolio: Tile and Stone
www.homeportfolio.com

Pratt and Larson
www.prattandlarson.com

Walker Zanger Tile
www.walkerzanger.com

Bedrooms

Bed Bath and Beyond
www.bedbathandbeyond.com

Chattam and Wells
www.chattamandwells.com

Charles P. Rogers
www.charlesprogers.com

Duxiana
www.duxiana.com

Garnet Hill
www.garnethill.com

Iron Bed
www.ironbed.co.uk

Linen Source
www.linensource.com

Pioneer Linens
www.pioneerlinens.com

Fabrics

Calico Corners
www.calicocorners.com

F. Schumacher
www.fschumacher.com

French Fabrics
www.french-fabrics.com

International Fabric Collection
www.intfab.com

Laura Ashley
www.lauraashley.com

Pierre Deux
www.pierredeux.com

Say Provence
www.sayprovence.com

Waverly
www.waverly.com

Faux Painting

Faux Like a Pro
www.fauxlikeapro.com

Faux Painting Links
http://interiordec.about.com
Search for "Faux"

Faux Store
www.fauxstore.com

Plaid Enterprises
www.plaidonline.com

Flooring

Alloc
www.alloc.com

Authentic Pine Floors
www.authenticpinefloors.com

Bamboo Floors
http://interiordec.about.com
Search for "Bamboo"

Bruce Floors
www.bruce.com

Edelman Leather Floor Tile
www.edelmanleather.com

Hardwood
www.hardwood.org

Leather Library
www.interiorsurfaces.com

Paris Ceramics
www.parisceramics.com

Pergo
www.pergo.com

Wide Plank Flooring
www.wideplankflooring.com

Furniture

Anthropologie
www.anthropologie.com

Baker Furniture
www.kohlerinteriors.com

Ballard Designs
www.ballarddesigns.com/

Bassett Furniture
www.bassettfurniture.com

Century Furniture
www.centuryfurniture.com

The Conran Shop
www.conran.co.uk

Country French Antiques
www.countryfrenchantiques.com

Country Swedish
www.countryswedish.com

Design Within Reach
www.dwr.com

Drexel Heritage
www.drexelheritage.com

Ethan Allen
www.ethanallen.com

FurnitureGuide.com
www.furnitureguide.com

Furniture Links on About.com
interiordec.about.com

Harden
www.harden.com

Henredon
www.henredon.com

Ikea
www.ikea.com

Kathy Ireland Home Collection
www.KathyIreland.com

Laura Ashley
www.lauraashley.com

Lillian August Collection
www.drexelheritage.com

Maine Cottage Furniture
www.mainecottage.com

McGuire Furniture
www.mcguirefurniture.com

Mitchell Gold
www.mitchellgold.com

Multi York
www.multiyork.co.uk

Pottery Barn
www.potterybarn.com

R.O.O.M.
www.room.se

Shabby Chic
www.shabbychic.com

Smart Furniture
www.smartfurniture.com

Spiegel Catalog
www.spiegel.com

Stickley
www.stickley.com

Thomasville Furniture
www.thomasville.com

Wesley Barrell
www.wesley-barrell.co.uk

Global Décor

See also *Fabrics and Furniture*

The Africa Store
www.theafricastore.com

eMosaique.com
www.emosaique.com

Eziba
www.eziba.com

Haiku Designs
www.haikudesigns.com

Morocco Interiors
www.moroccointeriors.com

Novika
www.novika.com

Rue de France
www.ruedefrance.com

Toscana
www.toscanaceramics.com

Zimmer and Rohde
www.zimmer-rohde.com

Hardware

Atlas Homewares
www.atlashomewares.com

GoKnobs.com
www.goknobs.com

Hardware Hut
www.thehardwarehut.com

Horton Brasses
www.horton-brasses.com

Restoration Hardware
www.restorationhardware.com

Home Office

See also *Furniture*

Herman Miller
www.hermanmiller.com

Ikea
www.ikea.com

Lizell Home Office Furniture
www.lizell.com

NY Sit4Less
www.nysit4less.com

Office World
www.officeworld.com

Kids' Rooms

Bellini Furniture
www.bellini.com

Bombay Kids
www.bombaykids.com

Bratt Décor
www.brattdecor.com

Ethan Allen "EA Kids"
www.ethanallen.com

For Mercy's Sake
www.mercysake.com

Kids' Rugs
www.kidsrugs.com

Links on Kids' Rooms
http://interiordec.about.com
Search for "Kids"

Pottery Barn Kids
www.potterybarnkids.com

Posh Tots
www.poshtots.com

Kitchen/Storage

Allmilmo
www.allmilmo.com

Alno Germany
www.alno.com

Blum International
www.blum.com

Bulthaup Kitchen Architecture
www.bulthaup.com

Caesarstone
www.caesarstone.com

California Closets
www.calclosets.com

Clive Christian
www.clivechristian.com

Crown Point Cabinetry
www.crown-point.com

Custom Inserts
www.custominserts.com

Frigo Design Refrigerator Panels
www.frigodesign.com

Grass America Drawer Dividers
www.grassusa.com

John Boos and Co.
www.johnboos.com/

Kallista
www.kallista.com

Kitchens.com
www.kitchens.com

Kitchen Cabinet Manufacturers Association
www.kcma.org

Kitchen Design and Resources
http://interiordec.about.com
Search for "Kitchen"

Kohler Co.
www.kohler.com

Knape and Vogt Storage Products
www.knapeandvogt.com

Ovis Kitchen Organizers
www.ovisonline.com

Poggenpohl
www.poggenpohl.co.uk

Siematic
www.siematic.com

Silestone
www.silestone.com

Smallbone
www.smallbone.co.uk

Specialty Stainless
www.specialtystainless.com

Wellborn
www.wellborn.com

Whitehaus Collection
www.whitehauscollection.com

Zodiaq
www.zodiaq.com

Lighting

Bellacor
www.bellacor.com

ELights.com
www.elights.com

Fixture Store
www.fixturestore.com

Lamps Plus
www.lampsplus.com

Lightolier
www.lightolier.com

Lighting Universe
www.lightinguniverse.com

More about Lighting
http://interiordec.about.com
Search for "Lighting"

Progress Lighting
www.progresslighting.com

Robert Abbey, Inc.
www.robertabbey.com

Shades of Light
www.shades-of-light.com

Solatube
www.solatube.com

Task Lighting Corp.
www.tasklighting.com

Moldings

Balmer Moldings
www.balmerstudios.com

Cumberland Woodcraft
www.cumberlandwoodcraft.com

Feldman Wood Products
www.feldmanwoodproducts.com

Fischer and Jirouch Plaster
www.fischerandjirouch.com

Millwork Products
www.millworkproducts.com

Style Mark Accents
www.style-mark.com

Style Solutions Inc.
www.stylesolutionsinc.com

Paint/Walls

Benjamin Moore
www.benjaminmoore.com

Decorate Today
www.decoratetoday.com

Dutch Boy
www.dutchboy.com

ePaintStore.com
www.epaintstore.com

Glidden Paint
www.glidden.com

Loose Ends
www.looseends.com

Paint Ideas
www.paintideas.com

PaintInfo.org
www.paintinfo.org

Paint and Paper
www.paint-paper.co.uk

Sherwin-Williams
www.sherwin-williams.com

Van Dyke's Restorers
www.vandykes.com

Virtual Painting
www.virtualpainting.com

Room Planning Sites

Bob Vila 3D Designer
www.bobvila.com/DesignTools/
index.html
*Register and plan a room online to see
results in 3D.*

Flexidesign.com
www.flexidesign.com
*Experiment with colors, wallpaper, or
borders, and view a 3D elevation. Try
FlexiSwatch tool for fabrics, too.*

Kohler's Virtual Bath Planner
www.kohler.com
*Create a virtual bath (or shower) online
using your room dimensions.*

See My Design
www.seemydesign.com
*Play all day on this site, trying color
combinations and paints.*

Silk Greenery

Silk Greenhouse
www.silkgreenhouse.com

Silk Plants Plus
www.1800sendsilk.com

Trees International
www.treesinternational.com

Slipcovers

Interior Decorating on About
interiordec.about.com
Search for "Slipcovers"

Potatoskins
www.potatoskins.com

Surefit
www.surefit.net

Todoes
www.todoes.com

Stenciling

Annie Sloan Shop
www.anniesloan.com

Jan Dressler
www.dresslerstencils.com

Goddess Designs
www.goddessdesigns.com

L.A. Stencilworks
www.lastencil.com

Mad Stencilist
www.madstencilist.com

Nature's Vignettes Stenciling
www.naturesvignettes.com

Royal Design Studio Stencils
www.royaldesignstudio.com

Stencil Planet
www.stencilplanet.com

Window Treatments

Bed Bath and Beyond
www.bedbathandbeyond.com

Country Curtains
www.countrycurtains.com/

Hunter Douglas
www.hunterdouglas.com

Kirsch
www.kirsch.com

Laura Ashley
www.lauraashley.com

Levolor
www.levolor.com

Pottery Barn
www.potterybarn.com

Restoration Hardware
www.restorationhardware.com

Rue de France
www.ruedefrance.com

Smith and Noble
www.smithandnoble.com

Spiegel Catalog
www.spiegel.com

Vesta Hardware
www.ivesta.com

Window Tinting Films

Solar Film
www.solarfilmco.com

Vista Window Films
www.vista-films.com